Building National Campaigns

Activists, Alliances, and How Change Happens

Oxfam GB, founded in 1942, is a development, humanitarian, and campaigning agency dedicated to finding lasting solutions to poverty and suffering around the world. Oxfam believes that every human being is entitled to a life of dignity and opportunity, and it works with others worldwide to make this become a reality. For further information about Oxfam GB's work, visit www.oxfam.org.uk.

Oxfam GB is a member of Oxfam International, a confederation of 13 organisations working together in more than 100 countries to find lasting solutions to poverty and injustice: Oxfam America, Oxfam Australia, Oxfam-in-Belgium, Oxfam Canada, Oxfam France – Agir Ici, Oxfam Germany, Oxfam GB, Oxfam Hong Kong, Intermón Oxfam (Spain), Oxfam Ireland, Oxfam New Zealand, Oxfam Novib (Netherlands), and Oxfam Quebec. For further information about Oxfam International, visit www.oxfam.org.

For further information about Oxfam's publishing, and online ordering, visit www.oxfam.org.uk/publications.

A companion website for this book is available at:
www.oxfam.org.uk/nationalcampaigns

This site contains further photos from the five case-study campaigns, video clips, campaigning materials, and a set of Powerpoint slides which summarise the contents of the book for presentations or for those coming to the issues for the first time.

Building National Campaigns
Activists, Alliances, and How Change Happens

Dave Dalton

Oxfam

Cover photo: Colombo, Sri Lanka: participants at a South Asia 'WE CAN' campaign assembly, each take a balloon for releasing outside the park.
(Annie Bungeroth/Oxfam)

First published by Oxfam GB in 2007

© Oxfam GB 2007

ISBN 978-0-85598-574-5

A catalogue record for this publication is available from the British Library.

The information in this publication is correct at the time of going to press.

Available from:

Bournemouth English Book Centre, PO Box 1496, Parkstone, Dorset, BH12 3YD, UK
tel: +44 (0)1202 712933; fax: +44 (0)1202 712930; email: oxfam@bebc.co.uk

USA: Stylus Publishing LLC, PO Box 605, Herndon, VA 20172-0605, USA
tel: +1 (0)703 661 1581; fax: +1 (0)703 661 1547; email: styluspub@aol.com

For details of local agents and representatives in other countries, consult our website:
www.oxfam.org.uk/publications
or contact Oxfam Publishing, Oxfam House, John Smith Drive, Cowley, Oxford, OX4 2JY, UK
tel +44 (0) 1865 472255; fax (0) 1865 472393; email: publish@oxfam.org.uk

Our website contains a fully searchable database of all our titles, and facilities for secure on-line ordering.

Published by Oxfam GB, Oxfam House, John Smith Drive, Cowley, Oxford, OX4 2JY, UK

Printed by Information Press, Eynsham
Inners printed on recycled paper made from 100% post-consumer waste.
Cover printed on FSC accredited 75% recycled paper.

Oxfam GB is a registered charity, no. 202 918, and is a member of Oxfam International.

Foreword

Women workers are an increasing part of the global labour force. They often find only poor-quality employment; as a result, they are working, but remain trapped in poverty. No matter the context, many women workers face multiple challenges. They may be young; they may be migrants; some are agricultural waged workers; some work at home; often they are isolated and do not belong to worker organisations; and their voices may be unrepresented in decision-making forums. Poor-quality employment creates inequality, and threatens sustainable development and gender equality.

Women's organisations, migrant-advocacy organisations and trade unions have developed many strategies to try to improve the conditions of women and migrant workers and to generate respect for their rights. These include worker education and awareness raising, protests against abuses, research, international solidarity, and worker organising. High-profile campaigning and alliance building have become important strategies for making change. Yet in many contexts, it is unclear to organisations how to campaign most effectively.

This book describes five campaigns in which Oxfam International (OI) supported existing national initiatives with global research on the relationship between trade, employment, development, and gender equality. Partners valued OI's capacity and experience in global campaigning, and the opportunity to strengthen links with campaigns on workers' rights in other countries. Those partners who had less experience in media work, developing policy proposals, lobbying, building alliances, or popular communications, were interested to learn how national campaigning could help achieve change.

In the end, the learning has been two-way. OI considers the national labour-rights campaigns to be innovative experiences. OI wanted to document learning on how these initiatives developed new ways of campaigning and overcame obstacles. Other partner organisations have also asked about the labour alliances' process, choices, problems, and successes, so that they can learn lessons for their own campaigns on agricultural policy and other areas. In late 2005, labour alliances in five of the 16 countries where OI has supported work on this issue agreed to do research and interviews for this book, although they are quick to point out that their campaigns are not necessarily 'better' than those of other national labour alliances.

These are stories of innovation and problem solving. This book does not cover all aspects of building national campaigns. We believe stories are a way of learning. These stories may not exactly match your own context or challenge, yet may help in thinking of new ways to overcome the obstacles you are facing.

The five campaigns described in this book operated in widely different circumstances, with different aims, on four continents (North and South), and within different industries. What they have in common is a passion for justice, the conviction that women have the power to make change happen, a commitment to hard work, and a track-record of persistence and creativity. They were all motivated by the belief that respect for labour rights is a way to help people overcome poverty and move toward greater gender equality. If your organisation is campaigning on women's labour rights or other justice issues, or thinking of doing so, we hope that you find ideas, lessons, and questions in this book that will help you to be even more effective. And if you are not, we hope that this book will inspire you to start.

Mary Sue Smiaroski
(Oxfam International Labour Rights Team)

Contents

Acknowledgements

This book was commissioned and project-managed by Mary Sue Smiaroski, written by Dave Dalton (Commonsense Communications (++ 44) 01748 829452), and based on case studies by the following people:

  Colombia: Myriam Bautista
  Morocco: Aspasia Papadopoulou
  Nicaragua: Joel Zamora
  Sri Lanka: Kalani Subasinghe
  USA: Roberto Lovato

This book would not have been possible without the assistance of: Ms Theja Godakandaarchchi and Ms Prema Gamage who helped conduct the interviews for the Sri Lanka case study; Ms Leticia Zavala for her extensive work facilitating access to the workers in the fields of North Carolina for the US case study; Sana Jelassi for her support and review of the case-study work in Morocco; and Thalia Kidder for her comments on the draft versions of the book.

With thanks to all the organisations that dedicated time to help the development of the case studies.

With thanks to the Oxfam affiliate staff who have supported the development of the labour-rights campaigns and the case studies documenting those experiences:

  Sonia Vila Hopkins – Morocco – Intermón Oxfam
  Pilar Rueda – Colombia – Oxfam GB
  Kalani Subasinghe – Sri Lanka – Oxfam Australia
  Roxanne Murrell – Nicaragua – Oxfam Canada
  Guadalupe Gamboa – USA – Oxfam America

The labour-rights campaigns received financial and other support from different Oxfam affiliates, including those outlined above as well as Oxfam-in-Belgium and Oxfam Novib and other international non-government organisations.

List of abbreviations

AFL-CIO	American Federation of Labor-Congress of Industrial Organizations: the trade-union federation of the USA
AlaRM	Apparel-industry Labour Rights Movement: the campaign alliance in Sri Lanka
ATC	Agreement on Textiles and Clothing: an agreement which set out the process of phasing out the Multi-Fiber Agreement
CDG	*Centre de Droits des Gens* (Centre for People's Rights): a member of the campaign alliance in Morocco
CGT	*Central General de Trabajadores* (General Workers Union): a member of the campaign alliance in Colombia
CTC	*Confederación de Trabajadores de Colombia* (Workers' Confederation of Colombia): a member of the campaign alliance in Colombia
CUT	*Central Unitaria de Trabajadores* (Unified Workers Union): a member of the campaign alliance in Colombia
FLOC	Farm Labor Organizing Committee: the organisation which led the campaign alliance in the USA
H2A	Section of US immigration law which allows workers holding H2A visas (also known as 'guest workers') to enter the country to work for a specific employer
HDI	Human Development Index
ILO	International Labour Organisation
INGO	international non-government organisation
INSS	Institute of Social Security in Nicaragua: a member of the campaign alliance in Nicaragua

MAS H2A   Anti-union employers' association in North Carolina, which opposes the NCGA's agreement with FLOC and fights unionisation in agriculture

MEC   *Movimiento de Mujeres Empleadas y Desempleadas María Elena Cuadra* (Maria Elena Cuadra Movement for Working and Unemployed Women): a member of the campaign alliance in Nicaragua

MFA   Multifibre Arrangement: an agreement which governed trade in textiles and garments between poor countries and rich countries

NCGA   North Carolina Growers' Association

NGO   non-government organisation

OI   Oxfam International: different affiliates from this international confederation of development agencies supported the national campaign alliances with funding, training, support and accompaniment, according to the alliances' needs and the context of the campaign

RSTN   *Red de Salud de los Trabajadores de Nicaragua* (Nicaraguan Network for Workers' Health)

TNC   trans-national corporation (or company): a business trading in more than one country; usually a business based in a rich country which also operates in poor countries

UMC   United Methodist Church (USA)

Introduction

Aim of this book

The aim of this book is to share stories and learning from alliance-based efforts to improve employment standards for workers, primarily women in export-orientated supply chains. These stories are about people and their organisations building more powerful and effective ways to get their voices heard. Anyone wanting to learn more about popular campaigning work, and about how change happens, will benefit from reading this book. It will show others who are working in this area how the initiatives it describes led to developing new campaigning components and overcoming obstacles. This book differs from a campaigning manual; the stories show how the relationships were developed and what processes were followed, explain the motivations behind the choices that the different alliances made, and highlight the resulting successes and failures of these alliances.

Oxfam International and the trade campaign

National and international non-government organisations are increasingly recognising the need to campaign for changes together with poor people and communities. Oxfam International (OI) is a growing confederation of autonomous non-government organisations (currently there are 13 affiliates), committed to working together and with local partners to fight poverty and injustice around the world. The members of the Oxfam 'family' have variously combined saving lives in emergencies, changing lives through development, and, more recently, changing policies through campaigning in order to respond to the challenge of poverty. In the text of the book, the word 'Oxfam' should be taken to mean Oxfam International or the relevant OI affiliate for the country under discussion.

Campaigning includes lobbying those in power – government, international organisations, and business – to change their policies or practice; mobilising large numbers of people in support of change – that is, persuading them to care, and to take action; and using the media to back up lobbying and mobilisation. Campaigns are based on information, knowledge, and analysis, which lead to practical proposals for better policies. In some countries, the government and politicians try to stop national organisations from being active, or even from existing. This makes it hard for organisations to acquire the necessary skills or implement successful campaigns. The campaigns Oxfam supports are non-violent, legal, and participative – working *with* poor, marginalised people, not *for* them.

In 2002 Oxfam launched its second global campaign – Make Trade Fair. This ambitious campaign identified the rigged rules and double standards underlying the system of international trade that keeps poor countries poor. The campaign focused on particular examples to help demonstrate the impact of trade rules on people living in poverty. These examples included: the low prices of commodities such as coffee, which kept poor producers poor; limited access to medicines due to patent rules; and the lack of respect for labour rights in the global supply chains of trans-national companies (TNCs). The campaign sought to put a human face onto the complex issue of international trade, identifying the underlying problems in the current system and ways to tackle these.

Oxfam also sought to connect international popular campaigning and advocacy on global policy with national advocacy and grassroots organising. This approach required understanding shared problems across a number of countries.

Labour rights

Having a job has long been thought of as a way to get out of poverty. In many cases, especially in poor countries, this is not true. People at work are often unable to lift themselves and their families out of poverty, and they remain trapped. In many economies the problem is mainly the lack of decent and productive work opportunities, rather than outright unemployment. Though trade rules are not the only problem, trade liberalisation has clearly played a role in changing this situation. As part of the Make Trade Fair campaign, Oxfam identified initiatives through which labour rights might be improved by undertaking campaigning work.

Together with partners, Oxfam carried out research in 12 countries to understand the causes of precarious employment of women and migrant workers in global supply chains. Precarious employment is characterised by:

- absence of contracts, short-term contracts, and part-time or seasonal work (but often also excessive hours);
- wages at or below the minimum wage, or unstable incomes through piece-rate pay or meeting quotas set by managers;

- little access to social-protection programmes (health insurance, maternity leave, etc.);
- little or no legislative protection; and
- no recognition of freedom of association[1] or the right to collective bargaining.

The research showed that it didn't matter which country you were in, or which industry you looked at, or even which type of government you had: the problem of precarious employment was the same, and it was growing. Commercial pressures and the advice of international institutions have weakened governments' ability to regulate the labour market. Changes in production methods, instability in industries, and precarious employment make it increasingly difficult for trade unions to operate. The purchasing and sourcing practices of TNCs undermine their own codes of practice, and they transfer risks down their supply chains. Governments roll back labour rights, and are cutting social programmes. So, the workers involved (primarily women) can't overcome poverty, because they are, in effect, subsidising the employers and the governments with their paid and unpaid (caring) work.

Oxfam believes that labour rights can be improved by combining four complementary change strategies:

- organising workers;
- changing ideas and beliefs;
- lobbying the private sector for an ethical business model (sourcing and purchasing practices); and
- lobbying governments to respect and defend labour rights and women's rights.

The labour-rights campaigns also changed the way Oxfam works with partners and allies. In many cases previously Oxfam had been regarded more as a donor that funded development programmes and supported civil-society initiatives. In the labour-rights campaigns Oxfam took on new roles that supported advocacy on labour rights at the national level, and campaigned to change trade rules and corporations' purchasing practices at the global level.

Gender equality

Women have been moving into the labour market in increasing numbers. With this movement, there have been changes in the relationships between men and women, both at work and at home. Work is paid, however inadequately. Caring and reproductive work is usually unpaid. At work and at home the opportunities and constraints are different for men and women.[2]

In 2004 Oxfam published a major report, 'Trading Away Our Rights',[3] which showed that international trade has drawn millions of women into employment across the developing world. They are producing the goods that are fuelling export growth – yet they are systematically denied a fair share of the benefits. International trade is wasting its potential.

The report showed how women workers pay hidden costs (when compared with men): out-of-pocket expenses, less pay for the same work, less opportunity for advancement, adverse impact on their health, and shorter working lives. In part, this is explained by gender-based discrimination: the widespread but incorrect belief that women's work has little economic value. Moreover, women's work caring for their families is often not valued either. But countries pay hidden costs too, with a workforce which is exhausted and often in poor health. And communities also pay hidden costs: women workers, putting in long hours at work, have less time to participate in community life, so communities lose their advocates. For these reasons, Oxfam is involved in the situation as a development agency, concerned with women workers' inability to overcome poverty and discrimination. That is why Oxfam chose to support labour-rights work, in the context of Make Trade Fair.

The case-study countries and partners

After discussions with various funded partners about the challenges of being part of a global campaign, taking on additional research, media work, and alliance building, various Oxfam affiliates agreed to support specific initiatives on labour rights in the following countries: USA, Honduras, Nicaragua, El Salvador, Guatemala, Colombia, Chile, UK, Morocco, Kenya, South Africa, Bangladesh, Sri Lanka, Indonesia, Thailand, Cambodia, and Hong Kong. While the labour initiatives in Kenya and Cambodia continue their work, these are now less connected with Oxfam campaigning. Oxfam has begun funding labour-rights initiatives in several other countries, including India.

This book looks at five different country campaigns, each primarily supported on the ground by a different Oxfam affiliate (see Table 1). In the cases of Sri Lanka and Colombia, funding was also provided by additional Oxfam affiliates. In Nicaragua, Oxfam affiliates had provided funding for an overall regional strategy, and the alliance there received a proportion of the total amount. In all these cases, the relationships were established and maintained as Oxfam collaborations. Finally, some of the campaigns received funding from other international organisations beyond Oxfam (see the 'Strengths' section in Chapter 2 for a discussion of funding).

Table 1: The five country campaigns

Country	Oxfam co-ordination	Additional Oxfam affiliate support
Colombia	Oxfam GB	Intermón Oxfam (Spain); Oxfam Novib (The Netherlands)
Morocco	Intermón Oxfam (Spain)	
Nicaragua	Oxfam Canada	Oxfam-in-Belgium; Oxfam GB; Intermón Oxfam (Spain); Oxfam Novib (The Netherlands)
Sri Lanka	Oxfam Australia	Oxfam America
USA	Oxfam America	Oxfam GB; Oxfam Novib (The Netherlands)

These five were chosen to be representative of the overall labour-rights campaigning work, in terms of geography, industries (garment industry and agriculture for export), types of problems and demands, and the array of Oxfam affiliates involved.

This book

The book describes and analyses what happened, and how it happened, in the five case-study countries. All faced enormous obstacles, and were able to overcome them through innovation, new ways of working in alliance, and patient persistence towards an end goal. This book is not intended to be an evaluation: rather it finds patterns of convergence or divergence between five very different campaigns. It documents experience which will be interesting and helpful to other campaigners on women's and migrants' labour rights. Campaigners working on other issues could usefully adopt the learning points and examples of good practice. The book does not contain a recipe for instant success, for several reasons: success in campaigning is rarely quick or complete; not everything described here was a success; and circumstances vary so much from place to place and from time to time. Rather than a recipe, what is offered here is a menu, from which the reader can pick whatever seems appropriate and helpful.

The book has been organised according to five critical factors that were especially relevant in the national labour-rights campaigns:

- building alliances;
- developing a strategy;
- incorporating a gender perspective;
- communicating the messages; and
- developing alternative policy proposals to solve problems.

There are many other important dimensions of campaigning which are not covered here. The book starts with the national contexts of the five case-study campaigns, and a brief outline of each campaign to set the scene. It then examines the campaigns under the five main headings mentioned above. This thematic approach, looking at campaigns from different aspects, inevitably leads to some overlap. Each section concludes with a list of key points that readers might consider for their own campaigns. Readers should also be alert, throughout the book, for ideas which are relevant to their own circumstances. In some places the text is not specific about persons, organisations, or countries, or changes names: this is to protect identities for reasons of security or privacy.

This book is dedicated to the people whose work it describes, to campaigners around the world whose creativity challenges old problems in new ways, and to women and migrant workers defending their rights everywhere.

1 • Contexts

The case-study countries compared

The statistics in Table 2 are intended to give a sense of the economic and social context in the countries where the case-study campaigns took place.

Table 2: The different contexts in the five countries

	Colombia	Morocco	Nicaragua	Sri Lanka	USA
Population (millions, 2003)	44.6	30.1	5.5	19.2	290.8
Life expectancy at birth (2003)	72	69	69	74	77
Gross National Income per capita (US$, 2003)	6,410	3,940	3,180	3,740	37,750
Human Development Index (HDI) ranking (out of 177)	69	124	112	93	10
Female % of labour force, 2003	39.7	35.2	38.2	36.1	46.6
Women in parliaments, % of total seats, 2004	12	11	21	4	14
Literacy (%, 2002)					
Male	92	63	77	95	99
Female	92	38	77	90	99

Source: The source for the HDI ranking is the UN Development programme [http://hdr.undp.org/statistics/data/hdi_rank_map.cfm]; the source for all the other statistics is the World Bank [http://devdata.worldbank.org/wdi2005/Section2.htm]

The Gross National Income figure is a rough measure of the wealth of the country. The difference between male and female literacy rates provides a rough measure of the position of women in society. The Human Development Index (HDI) focuses on three measurable dimensions of human development: living a long and healthy life, being educated, and having a decent standard of living. It combines measures of life expectancy, school enrolment, literacy, and income to allow a broader view of a country's development than does income alone. The smaller the number, the higher the country's HDI ranking.

Although the HDI is a useful starting point, it is important to remember that the concept of human development is much broader and more complex than any summary measure can capture, even when supplemented by other indices. The HDI is not a comprehensive measure. It does not include important aspects of human development, notably the ability to participate in the decisions that affect one's life and to enjoy the respect of others in the community.

Though not strictly comparable, due to differences in the years when the information was gathered in Table 2, it is useful to consider the Gini Co-efficient as a reflection of income inequality within each country. Of the 126 countries where data is available, where first place would reflect the best income equality, Sri Lanka comes in at 34, Morocco at 64, the USA at 73, with Nicaragua at 84, and Colombia towards the bottom at 118.[4]

The case-study campaigns

Colombia

The two years of the campaign in Colombia have coincided with the consolidation of a neo-liberal economic model and corresponding structural-adjustment policies which have reduced the social functions of the state and have fundamentally favoured the private sector. The country experienced 4.5 per cent growth in 2006 but poverty persists, with an estimated 45 per cent of the population living in poverty, of which 26.6 per cent are households headed by women. The negotiation of a free trade agreement with the USA has provoked significant opposition amongst different sectors of civil society due to concerns over its potentially negative effects on poverty and vulnerable groups. In general, civil-society organisations, including trade unions, carry out their activities in a hostile environment and their leaders have often been targeted, threatened, and killed as a result of the conflict. The International Labour Organisation considers Colombia to be the country where it is most dangerous to exercise trade-union rights. Current security policies which borrow ideas and language from the fight against 'terrorism' have contributed to a prevailing stigmatisation of social organisation and protest, which is often reflected in the elite-owned media.

Despite these challenges, civil-society organisations and social movements are strong and articulate, and continue to mobilise courageously around issues of concern.

A national alliance did not exist prior to the start of the campaign. There were some women's and human-rights organisations working on similar issues, and two partner NGOs with a great interest in trying to take advantage of Oxfam work on labour rights in supply chains (flowers for export) in the context of Make Trade Fair. Oxfam funded a co-ordinator post so that there would be someone working to bring the organisations together. In the context of conflict in Colombia (that involves lack of trust, and highly politicised environments), dedicated staff resources were important for helping this alliance to get up and running. It was especially important to hire someone who had a well-known reputation for working towards gender equality and respect for human rights.

The alliance has 57 members – trade unions, human-rights groups, women's organisations, and others – who have come together in a campaign under the slogan 'my rights are not negotiable'. The Oxfam-appointed co-ordinator played a facilitation role, taking responsibility for the minutes of meetings, dissemination of information, and so on. Although this role is key, the alliance has succeeded because it has promoted actions that strengthen the agenda of each participating organisation. The alliance focuses on the harmful effects of a labour-law reform passed in 2002, and uses mobilisation and media work to raise awareness of the harmful effects on women in particular. It also successfully opposed a change in women's retirement age, and it trained women workers. Women led the campaign, women's organisations were prominent in the alliance, and they learned to negotiate with male leaders of the trade unions about gender-equality issues. The political agreement of the campaign – to work from a women's-rights perspective – was key in order to overcome difficulties during internal negotiations about specific actions.

Morocco

Morocco is a constitutional monarchy, with an elected parliament. The king of Morocco has vast executive powers. The government is currently controlled by a centre-left coalition. Opposition political parties are legal and several have arisen in recent years, including a strong Islamist party. Morocco's media space is relatively open. The trade-union movement has existed since Morocco's independence in 1956, but has been weakened since neo-liberal reforms were introduced in the 1980s. There is a large and growing number of civil-society organisations campaigning on human rights (civil, political, social, economic, and cultural rights) and women's rights. A strong women's-rights movement was further emboldened in 2003 when the king proclaimed progressive reforms in Morocco's family law (thereby improving women's status in society).

An alliance of six organisations – trade unions, human-rights organisations, and women's organisations – campaigns under the name *Alliance pour les Droits des Travailleuses* (Alliance for Women Workers' Rights). The campaign is called *Campagne nationale pour l'application effective de la legislation du travail* (National campaign for labour-law enforcement). Oxfam played an important role in setting up and supporting the alliance. The campaign focuses on lobbying the government to implement a new national labour law passed in 2004 as a means to strengthen women's social and economic rights. Good contacts with the Moroccan employment minister and top officials are backed up by work in the media.

Nicaragua

Nicaragua has a democratic government; the most recent elections were held in November 2006. The previous government tended towards conservative policies combined with support for a neo-liberal agenda. It is too soon to know what the impact of the new government's policies will be. Over the last several years, one of the previous government's economic strategies had been to establish free trade zones in various parts of the country. Unlike most other countries in Central America, Nicaragua continues to receive new investments in this area. Between 2003 and 2004, exports increased by 28 per cent. Civil society is quietly thriving, and while most of civil society has adjusted to the new context following the defeat of the Sandinistas in 1990, trade unions continue to struggle. The unions have been under siege since 1990 for a variety of reasons: downsizing in the state; high unemployment; difficulties in adjusting to a new context (no state as protector); and in the case of the growing *maquila* sector, little gender analysis.[5]

NGOs and women's and farmers' organisations, while also facing challenges, have been better able to adapt to the new circumstances and have been more active in defending their rights and challenging policies or presenting proposals. The media has national reach, and though generally conservative, it does cover issues related to the free trade zones. Many organisations have denounced the lack of respect for labour legislation; however, it is a women's organisation which recognises the gendered relations in this sector, and in labour in general, and which works to improve women's rights.

A pre-existing alliance of ten organisations, including government ministries, universities, and labour organisations, led by a well-established women's organisation, took up the regional campaign for women workers' rights under the slogan 'employment yes – but with dignity'. Oxfam assumed a role of accompaniment – giving financial, research, and analysis support and adding weight. The alliance lobbied for new legislation on occupational health to the extent of drafting a bill; supported the lobbying by mobilisation and media work; and ran training courses for women workers. With acknowledged leadership by a women's organisation, gender equality was always a central concern of the campaign.

Sri Lanka

Sri Lanka, officially known as the Democratic Socialist Republic of Sri Lanka, is governed by an executive president. The government is investor-friendly, and media space is relatively open. Traditionally, the labour movement has been politically active, especially in the state sector. Union membership is subject to fluctuations because of competition among unions affiliated with different political parties, as well as a fairly rapid turnover of unions. At the time of the campaign, there existed diverse and progressive trade unions and women's organisations working with apparel-sector workers.

An alliance of 12 organisations – five trade unions, four labour organisations, and three 'observers' – campaigned under the name ALaRM (Apparel-industry Labour Rights Movement). Oxfam had a major role in forming and facilitating the alliance, which agreed on four campaign issues related to problems in the garment industry. The campaign included research, training and awareness raising, media work, mobilisation of women workers, and lobbying stakeholders. The different histories of working separately and individually created tensions between the members of the alliance.

USA

At the time of the campaign, the USA had a conservative, business-friendly, anti-labour government with a very weak opposition. The trade-union movement has had the challenge of adapting to a globalised economy and the loss of manufacturing jobs overseas. In some cases, churches and civil-society organisations have shared many of the roles traditionally played by the unions, including fighting against poverty and discrimination, and fighting for environ-mental justice and immigration reform. Migrant agricultural workers in the USA are excluded from national labour laws that grant industrial workers the right to organise and form labour unions. Due to this exclusion from collective bargaining laws, migrant workers have instead mobilised immigrant-labour organisations, labour, student, and community alliances to put pressure on employers to sit down and bargain collectively with their labour representatives.

Groups supporting the Mt. Olive boycott, ranging from churches to political parties, converge in the lead-up to the boycott anniversary on 17 March 2003, USA.
Source: Lori Fernald Khamala 2003

A loose and informal alliance led by a trade union campaigned for union recognition for male migrant farm workers. Oxfam has had an arm's-length role, helping with research and providing yearly grants and specific financial support at key moments. A network of supporters, including churches and students, organised a consumer boycott on a pickle company, Mt. Olive, which put pressure on the growers to negotiate with the union. The campaign became known as the Mt. Olive campaign. The mobilisation of consumers around the boycott was backed up by mobilising the workers, and culminated in a concerted effort, against a tight deadline, to get workers to sign up to the union. Although the workers are almost all men, the women in the alliance have played a prominent role and bring a gender perspective to the campaign.

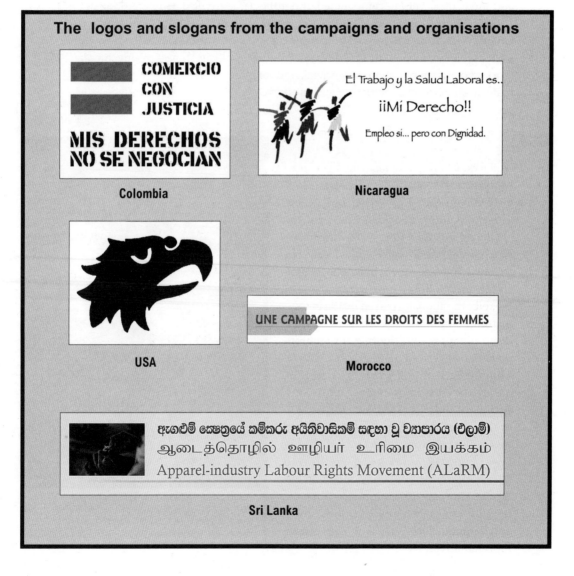

The logos and slogans from the campaigns and organisations

Colombia

Nicaragua

USA

Morocco

Sri Lanka

2 • Building an alliance

Overview

Strong alliances create good campaigns. Oxfam and its partners are promoting work in coalitions: they recognise that going it alone will not bring the changes that they need and want, and they are willing to make the effort and investment in building alliances. An alliance of existing organisations can benefit from the strength, experience, skill, contacts, and reputation of its members. In the process, members of the alliance can learn from one another, gain confidence, understand each other's limits, and increase mutual trust. But alliances need leadership; some members may have a history of competition and conflict; and tensions may arise in the operation of the alliance.

History

The organisations which joined or formed the alliances in the case-study countries all had a past, and a reason for being, before the alliance. Sometimes they had worked together in previous alliances for specific purposes. These alliances may have been more or less short-lived. At best the organisations had mutual respect and recognised each other's role and expertise.

Many organisations had a history of working on the issues (labour rights or women's rights or some combination), though perhaps not always together. Some had already developed working relations, though they tended to be short-term. Building an alliance to campaign on women's labour rights involved the members in new ways of working. In Morocco and Sri Lanka, these included shifting from opportunistic, short-lived campaigns to denounce problems, to developing joint longer-term, comprehensive advocacy strategies, and creating an alliance that included local organisations and an international actor such as Oxfam. In the case of Nicaragua, the alliance had worked together for a while, but it was the first time that they decided to work on a campaign together. In the USA, the campaign involved reactivating a pre-existing network of supporters and allies.

In Morocco, organisations in the alliance had lobbied parliament during the 1990s to ensure that women workers' specific needs were included in Morocco's first labour code. Unions in the alliance were directly involved in drafting the law and in negotiating its content through a dialogue with government and employers.

In Nicaragua the *Movimiento de Mujeres Empleadas y Desempleadas Maria Elena Cuadra* (MEC – Maria Elena Cuadra Movement for Working and Unemployed Women) is a well-established national women's organisation. In 2004, before the formation of the alliance, MEC had proposed a reform and additions to the law on Special Industrial Zones, and mobilised women workers to collect 50,000 signatures in support of the bill, which was approved unanimously by the National Assembly (the president later vetoed the law). As we will see below, this track-record gave MEC the undisputed leadership of the alliance, and was the forerunner of further impressive campaigning actions.

In the USA, the alliance was led by the Farm Labor Organizing Committee (FLOC), which had been organising farm workers since 1967. The alliance was rooted in work done with progressive churches during previous FLOC efforts like the campaign against food giant Campbell's Soup. More than a dozen of the key progressive church leaders across the country in that campaign were also involved in the campaign described here. In the USA consumer boycotts in support of labour-rights campaigns have a history going back to the 1960s.

In Colombia the alliance was newly formed, and although there had been no similar alliance in the past, many of the initial core group of organisations shared a commitment to the defence of human rights. The alliance was made possible by a political agreement: to develop activities in defence of women's labour rights as a strategic right, in order to overcome poverty and gender-based discrimination. Another important agreement was to define ways of working (building consensus) and responsibilities and rights as members of the alliance.

But sometimes the alliance brought together organisations which had been in conflict. It was the first time that many of the organisations in the Sri Lankan alliance had worked together in a long-term forum, as opposed to having occasional meetings with one another. Going through the process of identifying definite actions of common interest was a necessary learning process to build trust and confidence in the alliance and its different members. Labour organisations are very divided in Sri Lanka, and this campaign has given many actors the opportunity to overcome those divisions in a longer timeframe, beyond one-off events.

Leadership

Alliances need recognised leadership in order to form in the first place, to work effectively, and to grow in strength. This leadership may come from a local organisation. In Nicaragua, a broad range of state institutions and other actors recognised MEC as an organisation that generated proposals, contributed to finding solutions to problems, and promoted women's rights. This recognition enabled MEC to participate in several influential groups: Corporate Social Responsibility in Nicaragua; the National Council for Occupational Health and Safety; and the National Council for Economic and Social Planning, as well as other official entities. MEC was also a member of an established alliance, the *Red de Salud de los Trabajadores de Nicaragua* (RSTN – Nicaraguan Network for Workers' Health). So MEC's leadership role was to persuade the RSTN to adopt the campaign on women workers' rights, and to work together on it as an alliance. MEC played a predominant role in many of the operational aspects of the campaign.

It is important to distinguish between MEC's campaign initiatives, and those of the alliance, which will be discussed below. A proposed (and later adopted) employment policy with a gender-equality perspective was a MEC initiative. However, MEC feels that the alliance gave impetus to this work and helped get their proposals accepted more quickly. The alliance's main campaign initiative was the law for occupational health and safety.

In the USA, the leadership role was performed by an established trade union, FLOC. FLOC did not set up a formal alliance, but called upon the help of other organisations or constituencies as and when necessary, using contacts from earlier campaigns (some of which date as far back as 1967).

In other cases Oxfam, or another international NGO, played a leadership role. At times, the role was determined by the context, and at other times by the needs of the alliance. Oxfam staff promoted active facilitation or co-ordination in the alliances (Sri Lanka, Colombia) or acted as an independent convener. In the case of Nicaragua, Oxfam played a 'behind the scenes' support role. It occasionally played a more public role when it was necessary to show the link between the national campaign and an international initiative (for example at the launch) to give the national campaign more backing. The partner in Nicaragua reported that the international link was appreciated.

In Colombia, the Oxfam Advocacy and Communications Officer played a key role in stimulating and bringing the alliance together, and acted as a co-ordinator of the campaign. Her strengths were her knowledge of, and relationship with, national organisations, and also that she is well-known as a defender of women's rights. She, in turn, found two key collaborators and allies: an expert on labour-rights advocacy who was recruited as part of the campaign team within Oxfam, and a staff member from an Oxfam partner organisation, Cactus, which works with women in the cut-flower industry and which had participated in the original research for the Oxfam report 'Trading Away Our Rights'. The personal and institutional links of this team helped draw together the 14 core members of the alliance. In Colombia there are many strong organisations and there is a lot of conflict and mistrust between them, resulting from the history of social and political violence in the country. So it was important to have a co-ordinator who was linked to an international organisation that could play a convoking and co-ordinating role. Another important aspect was Oxfam's decision to be just one more organisation on the co-ordination committee (to encourage shared decision-making and joint leadership) as well as to promote national public leadership skills amongst all the organisations.

Elsewhere, Oxfam's role was somewhat more proactive in getting the alliance and the campaign up and running. In Morocco, Oxfam joined three of its partners – *Centre de Droits des Gens* (CDG – Centre for Human Rights), *Association Marocaine des Droits des Femmes* (AMDF – Moroccan Association for Women's Rights), and the *Ligue Démocratique des Droits des Femmes* (LDDF – Democratic League for Women's Rights) – to launch the 'Trading Away Our Rights' report in February 2004. This event marked the start of a first alliance, which carried out several joint campaign activities over the following months. In October of that year, Oxfam recruited a campaign co-ordinator, who approached three more organisations on behalf of the initial alliance to see whether they were interested in joining the campaign. Oxfam's active role in co-ordinating the campaign in Morocco was determined by the needs of the alliance. In practical terms, nobody had time to take on the campaign's co-ordination, because all the members had full-time jobs and were active either in other civil-society initiatives or in political parties. Members also felt that it was appropriate for Oxfam to co-ordinate because it was seen as a neutral actor which didn't have any stakes in the campaign. Members feared that giving the co-ordination role to one of the members at the start could have politicised the campaign or raised tensions. The co-ordinator needed to go to organisations one by one to invite them to join the alliance, and this required personalised approaches and time to build relationships. Here, as elsewhere, Oxfam wanted to encourage local organisations to work together without becoming dependent on Oxfam's support, and it is a good sign that the alliance drafted a project proposal in March 2006 to raise funds for the campaign from another donor.

In Sri Lanka, Oxfam brought together the organisations which formed the alliance, and continued to play an active role in facilitation and co-ordination. Oxfam provided research and translation into the local language. Here, as in Morocco, Oxfam provided funding and acted as a facilitator to bring together disparate groups and help them reach consensus on campaign strategies. Because Oxfam comes from outside the country, it was seen as unbiased and impartial.

As a final point on leadership, it is important to note that in the cases of Nicaragua, Colombia, and Morocco, women led the alliance-building process, even in mixed organisations. This has been important in order to make women visible as social actors, as well as to allow them to articulate their needs and the effects of employment practices on their lives. To become leaders, women had to develop skills to be in the public sphere, which, due to gender discrimination, is not easy. The campaign has been a good empowerment process for women to get access to the mainly male political world. Leadership develops by doing. Women develop skills, while the members of the organisation, and the wider public, see women taking leadership roles. Women are capable of successfully leading alliances, and women's leadership is important to ensure a gender perspective.

Membership

Organisations join alliances in order to support the cause of the campaign and to reinforce their own organisation's efforts in the same area. In other words, they feel that the campaign is complementary to their own work. Smaller organisations may also feel that being a part of the alliance will enhance their profile and provide them with visibility at national and international level. Being part of an alliance is seen as a give-and-take relationship.

In the process of forming the alliance, and thinking about inviting new members to join, members asked questions such as: who do we need, to get the change we want? Who can open the doors? Who can provide research? Who knows journalists? In Nicaragua, it was a matter of inviting existing members of the network to become more active. In Morocco, the alliance asked questions at the beginning, and they continue to be raised as the alliance realises the need to mobilise a whole range of actors to deliver change. The key questions that the alliance is asking are: how do we prioritise whom we build strategic alliances with? Do we have time to build those relationships? Who takes responsibility for building them? The alliance is also still inviting key actors to be members.

There are wide variations in the kinds of organisations making up these alliances, but the most common elements are trade unions and women's organisations. Traditionally, these organisations have little history of joint work; in some notable cases, the history that does exist is laced with antagonism. Historical antagonism between organisations is unfortunately very common. It is divisive, and it is not always clear why the antagonism exists or how to resolve it. The reasons could be many (personalities, concern about not being able to lead the campaign, ideological differences, different priorities), but the antagonism is usually based on some experience, and only through other shared experiences will it be overcome.

It would be too easy to underestimate the work that went into bringing these organisations – with their different constituencies, different or even rival sources of funds, and different working and leadership styles – to sit down at a table together. Oxfam started its labour-rights work in Sri Lanka by inviting all organisations that were working on labour issues to join it. Organisations that showed an interest in this type of long-term campaign work, and which attended the meetings continuously, automatically became the 'core group'. This group consisted of five trade unions, four labour NGOs, and three 'observers'. The alliance began by extending invitations to other actors that they knew in the field, and they are still in the process of inviting new members to join, to make the alliance as inclusive as possible.

In the USA, FLOC drew on the help of university students, churches, and the national trade-union umbrella organisation AFL-CIO. In Nicaragua, RSTN included universities in Nicaragua and Italy (note that this is a partnered 'sister' relationship), government ministries, the Pan American Health Organization, and a trade union. The Moroccan alliance consisted of two women's organisations, two trade unions, and two human-rights organisations. And, as we have seen, sometimes Oxfam was a member of the alliance (in Sri Lanka and Morocco), and sometimes was at arm's length, either as a supporter of the organisation which was leading the alliance (in Nicaragua and the USA), or simply by commissioning the co-ordinator (in Colombia).

There is wide variation in the number of organisations within each alliance. There were six members in Morocco, and there is further discussion below of an attempt to expand the alliance there. At the other extreme, the alliance in Colombia grew to 57 members. Numbers are important, but as described below, the quality of relationships may be at least as critical in order to achieve change. The growth in Colombia should be seen as evidence of the success of the leadership and the core group. They organised launches in several major cities (not just the capital), and they specifically reached out to organisations beyond the usual collaborators and those already committed. As a result, the alliance includes women's organisations, human-rights organisations, development organisations, trade unions, labour NGOs, youth groups from universities, and grassroots women's leaders.

While this analysis focuses on organisations, it is individuals who do the work and form the relationships. In one exceptional case, an individual was effectively a member of the alliance in a personal capacity. Angelita Morrisroe, a former farm worker, is a member of the Latino community and the owner of a small grocery store, *La Palmita*, in Dudley, North Carolina. FLOC's first office location in the community was a small room behind the store. The pool table at *La Palmita* served, at different times, as a FLOC desk, press-conference location, meeting centre, and entertainment site for workers. FLOC organisers often took the opportunity to talk to workers who were waiting to make phone calls in the shop. All this was possible because Angelita supported the campaign, and she later donated a plot of land that currently houses the organisation.

Decision-making

All the alliances had 'endless' conversations, individual discussions, meetings, and workshops, to come to agreement about the campaign strategy. The decision-making process seemed to be consensual in each of these campaigns.

In Sri Lanka there were in-depth discussions, and a clear, informed analysis of all the options available. The alliance in Morocco felt that building consensus was essential to working as an alliance. There was no other way to ensure that all members got involved in organising joint activities. In the case of Nicaragua, there was no explicit decision that 'all our decisions will be by consensus' but it was understood, especially by MEC, that this was the way of working that would build support.

Consensus contributed to strengthening the alliance and building trust, as well as making decisions about strategy. In the Colombian case the consensual approach was a conscious political decision to provide reassurance to each member of the alliance. In the opinion of the alliance, this consensual approach cannot be separated from the fact that most of the active individuals were women. The individual people who were involved were also committed even beyond their institutions (a 'militant' commitment), even those in Oxfam. There are specific ways for women to participate and to build alliances, and these ways are often different from men's ways. Because they have experienced discrimination, those women who have analysed and reflected on its causes are more careful to ensure that they do not practise it themselves, and take conscious efforts to avoid a replication of this attitude in themselves. In practice, this results in them as leaders consulting the membership more often, being more conscious of process, taking step-by-step approaches, working longer to reach consensus, sharing leadership profiles, and other inclusive practices. It means that things may move more slowly, but the group moves as a group. This is not sexist: it does not mean that women's ways to build alliance are better than men's ways.

The style of decision-making within each alliance reflected its origins and leadership. Where there was a clearly recognised leading organisation, as in the USA, then decision-making could be informal. It might be internalised within the leading organisation, so that communication with allies takes the form of requests or suggestions to take actions that have already been decided by the leading organisation. The leadership style of FLOC within its informal alliance, for instance, was not consensual, in that FLOC is well-established and responds to its members, not to its allies.

In Colombia, 14 organisations within the alliance made up a core group which acted as a co-ordinating committee for the campaign. The co-ordinating committee could lead the decision-making, but this then had to be ratified by all members of the alliance before implementation. Every six months there were evaluation and planning meetings involving the wider alliance at which the strategic direction and action plan were defined. The co-ordination committee would then meet on a weekly basis to discuss how to carry out the plan and to monitor its implementation.

Although the alliance in Nicaragua had a clearly recognised leader, the alliance established an executive committee. This committee was in charge of planning activities, assigning responsibilities to other members of RSTN, and monitoring and supervision to ensure that the action plan was carried out.

The newly established alliances in Sri Lanka and Morocco had more formal decision-making processes. The alliance in Morocco, for instance, held strategic meetings every three months to agree on a plan of action, and organised other *ad hoc* meetings to prepare specific actions. Members also needed to follow up continuously with one another by email. All the members had a permanent representative to the alliance, and some had a vice-representative who supposedly followed the course of the campaign. (However, this system did not really work, as vice-representatives were not necessarily plugged into the campaign's discussions.) Members reported internally to their superiors. The minutes of meetings, circulated to all members, were the cornerstone of the alliance's work and served several purposes: they helped to keep track of the development of the alliance strategy and actions; they helped to set targets and prepare a plan of action; they were a reminder of the debates that had taken place, the decisions that had been made, and the points that members had agreed on; they were a binding reference document for all (this prevented members from deviating from the agreed points, which they found was always a possible risk); and finally, they ensured proper follow-up by members and their directors and prevented misunderstandings.

Trust

Mutual trust is essential to the effective working of an alliance. If each member agrees with the alliance's strategy and policy position, and if it feels that other members are making a fair contribution, it will enthusiastically contribute what it can to the campaign. Working in alliance helps each organisation to understand the institutional language and the institutional limits of the others, so they learn what they can actually ask and expect of each other.

In Colombia, members of the alliance carried out tasks according to their expertise, but also shared their skills with other members. As a member of the alliance commented:

> *It has been possible to consolidate a space characterised by trust, an essential ingredient to create alliances of any kind. A space where organisations with experience on labour-rights advocacy have shared their expertise to the benefit of those of us who did not have any experience in that field.*

In Morocco, all the members of the alliance benefited from advocacy training provided by Oxfam, which was an opportunity to share past campaigning experiences and to learn about how to build effective advocacy strategies as a group. In Sri Lanka, the members of the alliance agreed a general approach to running training programmes for workers, to be run by members individually and in some instances collectively.

In its role as alliance co-ordinator in Morocco, Oxfam actively tried to defuse tensions in order to create an environment of trust where members could work together. Ensuring that decision-making rules were clear and respected by every member, that agreements and commitments were honoured, and that everyone had the same information simultaneously, helped build this trust.

As in any group of organisations, the need for consensus means that sometimes one member's idea is overruled. It is a sign of growing trust that the member takes this philosophically.

Mutual support between members of an alliance also fostered trust. In Colombia, women's organisations supported the women's departments of trade unions in their shared efforts to increase the unions' awareness of gender-equality issues. The most important thing is that everybody feels that each person in the campaign can act as a representative of the common interests. Even in this atmosphere of trust and mutual respect the ground rules specified that completed activities would be evaluated 'so that mistakes could be corrected and that there would not be too much boasting about achievements'.

In the USA, FLOC worked with local church leaders to take the boycott demand to their national conventions. In Nicaragua, the members of the alliance worked together to provide training to workers in the *maquilas*. In the process the members of the alliance got to know one another better and increased their mutual respect.

It is impressive that alliances formed, held together, and developed mutual trust, considering their members' previous experiences. In most of the case-study countries there was little history of joint work between women's organisations and trade unions; and if there was, it was often antagonistic. The tensions exist due to turf wars: labour rights are seen exclusively as the domain of trade unions and women's rights are seen exclusively as the domain of women's organisations. There was also competition for funding, and differing analyses about the importance of women's rights, among other points. In almost all the cases, it was the first time that these organisations had come together to form an alliance to work on one common issue: women workers' labour rights.

Achieving agreement on strategy and policy was often a slow and difficult process, as we will see in later sections. Disparate organisations, each with their own agenda, perhaps unfamiliar with one another, or even with a history of rivalry, had to make compromises.

Differences among organisations may also get in the way of attempts to recruit new members of the alliance. In one country, alliance members invited a women's organisation to join. The organisation said that it was interested, but expressed reservations about 'what women's organisations have to say in a campaign about labour'. Alliance members speculated that the organisation might have felt uncomfortable with joining a campaign that had already been defined and run by other organisations for some time.

In Sri Lanka each member had an issue they felt passionately about, one on which their organisation was working, and each pressed for that to be the issue to be selected. Yet none of them dared to criticise or objectively analyse the relative importance of each of the issues. They felt that such an analysis would require critically looking at the activities and impact of other partners, and were not comfortable doing it in the forum. It took much encouragement from Oxfam for the members to debate openly enough to agree on common positions. The alliance invested heavily in turning the core group (who initially only came together when Oxfam asked them to) into an effective alliance that would engage in campaigning, sustain local pressure over a longer period, and continue to do so even after Oxfam reduces the scale of its intervention.

The work each member puts into the alliance is usually additional to the work the organisation is already doing. This creates an internal tension within each member organisation: how much time and energy can the organisation's staff spare for alliance work, and at the expense of which other priority? It also creates tensions between members if some feel that they are doing more than their fair share and others are doing less. In Sri Lanka, for instance, some members of the alliance devoted more time to AlaRM-related work, while others remained as nominal members. Nonetheless, the representation of national-level unions was appreciated, given the opportunities and credit they provided to the alliance, even though their time input was limited.

Perhaps the best that can be hoped for, in a newly established alliance, is the position in Morocco, where working within an alliance has given members the opportunity to find common ground on a number of issues.

Members acknowledged that even though they may not agree on all points, they have managed to keep their differences from affecting the campaign. As one member remarked:

'This is the first time a coalition has lasted for that long...political rivalries usually result in a coalition falling apart after a few months'.

One source of tension within the alliances, the different understandings of gender-equality work, is discussed in a later section.

Strengths

The strength of an alliance comes from the strengths of its members and working relationships. These vary from one organisation to another, but they can include:

- knowledge of and information about a particular policy area or a particular social group;
- a constituency of members or supporters;
- skill and experience in research, campaigning, or media work;
- reputation and respect from the government, other NGOs, the media, external donors, and the wider public.

Any one member of the alliance is unlikely to have all these strengths, and the ideal is for the alliance to bring together organisations with complementary strengths. In Nicaragua and Morocco, where the campaign focus was on women workers' rights, the strengths of trade unions and women's organisations were obviously complementary.

Trade unions have knowledge and experience of working with the labour force (often largely men) to defend their rights at work. Women's organisations have knowledge and experience of working with and for women to raise their awareness and confidence and defend their rights.

In Colombia the strengths of human-rights and women's organisations were complementary. In the USA, when FLOC wanted to mobilise large numbers of people to support a boycott, it approached churches to reach a different constituency of people. People who might not feel sympathetic to a boycott call coming from a trade union, would take notice because it came from their church.

In addition to these strengths of national organisations, Oxfam brought other strengths: necessary funding; help in drawing the alliance closer together; help in policy making by providing research and facilitating discussion; training; and bringing profile as an international organisation. The other alliance members, especially in Morocco and Sri Lanka, appreciated these strengths. An alliance member in Morocco said:

'If the government hears that this campaign is part of a global campaign, that we are bringing this to an international level, they will feel more pressured, they will react. Oxfam's involvement in the alliance helps make this more international'.

All the members of the alliance in Morocco saw it as an advantage that their campaign was put in the context of a global campaign for women workers' rights and that Oxfam was running a parallel campaign in Spain to improve Spanish companies' purchasing practices in Morocco. It reinforced their own campaign in the government's eyes, and enriched their campaign through lessons learned and experiences gained elsewhere. It also added a sense of solidarity with other campaigns – 'we are not alone in this'. Occasionally meeting with Oxfam staff involved in other campaigns and countries has helped members to get an idea of what is happening elsewhere, and to exchange views.

On the other hand, it may be a disadvantage if the campaign is seen, or can be presented by opponents, as being brought in from the outside. In Colombia, Oxfam staff were careful to keep a low profile, never taking leadership roles at public events, in order to make it clear that the campaign belonged to Colombian people and organisations. Oxfam felt that it would strengthen the leadership qualities of members of the alliance if they, not Oxfam, were spokeswomen for the campaign; it was also a strategy to build the capacities of the national organisations.

In Nicaragua, Oxfam funded various aspects of the campaign, including research, media work, awareness raising, and advocacy activities. Although Oxfam was not a member of the alliance, its support for MEC gave a little extra profile and credibility to MEC, and hence to the campaign which MEC led.

In the USA, Oxfam funded research on supply chains in agriculture. This demonstrated the downward pressure on workers' wages exerted by major profit-driven buyers, and validated FLOC's choice of Mt. Olive as the best target for the consumer boycott campaign. In addition to providing information for the 'Trading Away Our Rights' report, Oxfam published its own research under the title 'Like Machines in the Fields'. FLOC was featured in this report, and this gave FLOC added credibility in its work with national church organisations. Oxfam also provided a grant to hire organisers during the limited time period that FLOC had to sign up 8,000 workers to gain recognition as the collective bargaining agent.

In Sri Lanka the unique feature of the alliance is the collective implementation of activities, which further strengthens the alliance itself and also generates more recognition for ALaRM. Many partner organisations engage in collective activities, each partner pooling their resources at different times and levels, demonstrating the force that could be generated with the mobilisation of various resources. Inclusive-ness in research work and dissemination of findings enabled all organisations in the same sector to make use of information gathered by one organisation, breaking new ground in a field where each one was fighting for survival.

Research

The importance of research in policy making is discussed later. But it should be mentioned here because of its critical role in building alliances. Tensions between organisations in an alliance can be based on their differing analysis of a problem or its solution. Doing research together and agreeing on findings can establish common ground, even if different political perspectives remain. If one international NGO had done the research independently, this common ground and analysis might not have been established in the national alliances.

In the USA, the research (and as noted earlier its publication as an independent report) was helpful in getting the message out and recruiting supporters, because it gave the organisations credibility. In Sri Lanka, the research from a worker perspective gave the alliance recognition both among their own members and from others. The research-backed analysis helped them to lobby stakeholders, and contrasted with previous occasions when organisations simply made demands without any research backing. In Colombia, research served as a starting point to build the necessary political process for alliance members to come to agreement on the underlying analysis of the problem. In Nicaragua, it wasn't the first piece of research that they had done; MEC's usual practice of doing research when funds allow had helped them build up their credibility. The national research carried out by Oxfam in Morocco for 'Trading Away Our Rights' and as a basis for campaigning on corporate social responsibility in Spain (specifically targeting Spanish clothing companies sourcing in Morocco) positioned Oxfam in Spain's debate about corporate social responsibility – but did not necessarily help build the alliance in Morocco. However, the fact that Oxfam had developed expertise on the impact that clothing companies' purchasing practices had on women workers' rights in Morocco, gave Oxfam an 'added value'. Alliance members were very aware of the role that corporations play in undermining labour rights and found an ally in Oxfam, who had influence over, and access to, companies sourcing in Morocco. Targeting multinational corporations was seen as the 'missing link' in previous efforts to defend labour rights at the national level – working in an alliance with Oxfam opened up new channels to reach corporations.

Funding

Campaigning costs money. There were several ways in which the different Oxfam affiliates, partners, and alliances made decisions about who gets funds, and the transparency of the funding. In Sri Lanka, once the campaign strategy was identified, each alliance member knew about each other's activities and the amount of money that Oxfam was contributing to carry out the work. In Nicaragua, funding was channelled through the primary partner, MEC. But the campaign budget was presented quite transparently to the alliance and at a press conference. Transparency is important in building trust; one of the most damaging things to organisations or alliances can be rumours about how much money comes in and how it is used. The other organisations carried out their actions according to their own budgets. In the USA, only FLOC received funds, as others were network volunteers. During the urgent one-month sign up, they appealed for special funding to hire organisers, and Oxfam supported that initiative.

At the start of the campaign in Morocco, Oxfam funded one of its partners (CDG) to carry out a range of campaign activities – round-table discussions, t-shirts, press conferences, and so on. Once the co-ordinator was in place and the alliance enlarged, Oxfam managed the budget. There was no discussion about the amount of money available or a planning exercise about how funds would be spent – but it was made clear from the start that Oxfam would support the campaign both financially and through providing capacity-building support (training, advice, overall co-ordination); and that the budget was not very big. The alliance defined three-month action plans, and if any of the activities required funding, Oxfam would cover the cost. As the campaign moved forward, the alliance responded to opportunities to get further funding from other donors by drafting a proposal for future work.

For smaller, less well-funded organisations, the fundamental issue is about the opportunity costs of campaigning and advocacy. See the Resources section for further information on fund-raising.

Summary

At their best, alliances create the conditions for effective campaigning by bringing together the complementary strengths of their member organisations. Alliances can be important to establish common ground for the future and an experience of achieving a change – however small – together. If an existing, established alliance includes appropriate organisations and shares your perspective, it is worth trying to persuade it to adopt your campaign. The important exercise is to analyse the dynamics of change, considering your power analysis: who do you need to open doors, to have greater legitimacy, how will you reach the decision-makers? Who wants to work on this change with you? To create a new alliance needs leadership, and leadership must extend to fostering mutual trust to keep the alliance together. Oxfam or another international NGO may provide this leadership, or a local NGO may do so. It's important to remember that the development of an alliance is rarely straightforward; there will be progress and setbacks, moments of strength and weakness, throughout the entire life of the group. The key is to keep the goal in mind in order that all members remain motivated to work towards its achievement. Time and energy devoted to nurturing the alliance is well-spent; once established, the alliance can start to deliver effective campaigns and the international NGO can take a reduced role.

Membership of the alliance will depend on the campaign theme and the history of the organisations that have been working on the issue. The working of the alliance may be formalised, with regular, minuted meetings and written policy positions; or it may be a flexible arrangement between a lead organisation and allies which are called in to help as and when needed. As much as possible, members should contribute similar amounts of effort and receive equal amounts of credit for the work of the alliance as a whole. All the alliance-building efforts were, and still are, evolving; some alliances are strategic, others are tactical, and both approaches are important in the appropriate moments.

Key points

- Choose your allies carefully, taking into account your respective experiences. It is not only about increasing the numbers of members, but ensuring that each brings complementary strengths to the partnership.

- Carry out joint research and agree on findings to establish common ground between alliance members. Think about how research can strengthen the alliance as well as contributing to the development of policy proposals.

- Be aware of any personality clashes or historical disagreements between organisations that you may want to work with.

- Be ready to make compromises on strategy and policy.

- Ensure that decision-making rules are clear and respected by all.

- Take minutes of meetings and circulate them to members to ensure that there is a clear record of debates and decisions and to reduce the risk of later disagreements.

- Be aware of local attitudes and beliefs: your target audiences may be more sympathetic to information from one source (for example a church) than another (for example a trade union).

- Account for funds in a transparent way: this is essential to foster trust.

3 • Developing a strategy

Overview

A campaign strategy describes:

- what the problem is that you want to solve;
- what changes in policy and practice you want to achieve;
- whom you have to influence or convince to make those changes, and how you can communicate with them;
- whom you can look to for support, and how you can reach them;
- what actions you will take – and when the campaign is carried out by an alliance, which member of the alliance is responsible for which action and when.

The strategy should give you a vision of how people's lives will be different once the campaign goals are achieved.

Starting from here

In practice, the process of developing a strategy may not follow the sequence outlined above. Initially, the alliances' strategies were often limited to a launch event (commonly, a press conference). Only later did the alliances develop a fuller more in-depth strategy, through the identification of opportunities, sometimes using tools such as power analyses. Only in one case did the alliance actually sit down and write out a formal strategy. In particular, changes in the external environment may provide the stimulus or opportunity to create a campaign. The Make Trade Fair campaign's interest in supporting research on labour-rights issues was one such stimulus for building alliances and campaigning.

In Morocco, the government adopted a new labour code in June 2004 after more than 40 years of preparation. After carefully analysing the code's strengths and weaknesses, the alliance identified five provisions that, if adequately enforced, could help improve women workers' lives: an increase in the minimum wage, shorter weekly working hours, new health and safety committees in factories, a new medical service for workers, and restrictions on the use of temporary contracts. These five points became the key demands of the Moroccan campaign. The alliance could be said to have jumped directly to the 'solution' and 'target' stages of strategy development.

In Sri Lanka, the alliance members discussed their capacity, in terms of skills and resources, and what they thought they could achieve during the time period. They also started from a rights-based approach, which helped the alliance understand where, when, and how to campaign, what strategies to put in place, and to mobilise and network accordingly. They identified duty-bearers at different levels beyond the traditional trade-union identification of tripartite members (workers, government, and employers), extending to multi-stakeholders including buyers and other important local and international actors in the apparel industry. They demanded accountability and transparency from duty-bearers. By approaching the needs of the workers from a rights perspective, all action on behalf of workers was based on their rights as a matter of law, not simply on the fact that they needed a certain type of response. Alliance members also tried to think of a strategy that would build workers' capacity.

Some campaign strategies were developed by identifying what all the allies could agree on. Also, in addition to developing a sophisticated analysis of the problem, partners and allies prioritised what could be won (sometimes just a small piece of the analysis), which allowed the alliance to move beyond analysis to something that could have a concrete result. For instance, the alliance in Morocco decided to focus on five points in the labour code, rather than calling broadly for the whole labour law to be enforced. They have now learnt that even asking for five points is too ambitious and that, if they want to see change and monitor it, they would need to focus on only one very specific point.

Another important aspect of 'starting from here' is the ideas and beliefs of the alliance members and the wider society. Most allies and partners shared the same ideas and beliefs about labour-rights issues. But they did not always have the same consensus about gender discrimination and poverty. Some alliances had to spend time talking about women workers' labour rights, and why they are such a strategic issue, to deepen and balance the understanding among all members. Nonetheless, all knew that there were ideas and beliefs in the wider society that had to be changed, and included efforts to do so as part of their campaign strategy.

Examples of common myths in Morocco, Colombia, Sri Lanka, and Nicaragua are: women's work is less valuable than men's work; women workers' wages are 'pocket money' so they do not need to be paid much. In addition, in many areas of the world, some people believe that: women working in factories are prostitutes; women workers do not have the right to organise; women workers need men's permission to sign a contract; mothers or pregnant women should not be working; only unmarried women should work; employers cannot afford to abide by labour law in the current economic crisis, especially in the clothing and textiles sector; and union activity drives investors away.

In the USA, most people generally know the situation that farm workers face, at least on an intellectual level. But that wasn't enough. FLOC decided to promote personal contacts with workers so that people that they wanted as supporters could make a personal, emotional connection to the issue.

Identifying the problem

More commonly, the stimulus for a campaign is a problem. In Colombia the starting point was a labour law of 2002 (Law 789) which increased the precarious situation of women workers, so the alliance took up the challenge of rolling back this law (see Box 1).

Box 1: Law 789

Before the law changed in 2002, the basic working day was set from 6am to 6pm. After 6pm, the hours worked were paid as 'nocturnal' labour, at an overtime rate 75 per cent higher than daily hours. A substantial portion of the female labour force who worked in factories, restaurants, hotels, or as seamstresses, increased their earnings by working until 10pm. Law 789 extended the working day from 6am to 10pm. At the same time, the law decreased by 25 per cent the overtime that workers received on account of their hours worked on Sundays and holidays. The effect of these changes was that women's monthly salary was reduced by 14.5 per cent on average, so that their current income barely covered 45 per cent of the cost of the official 'market basket' of necessary goods.

As a result, women had to work longer hours, more often on weekends and holidays, to bring their earnings up to the level they had before the law changed. A case study carried out with 113 workers within the formal sector of the economy concluded that after the change in the law, 26 per cent of women were adding work in the informal economy, such as street selling, to their formal work to make up for their loss in income. Also, all of these women use their free time, or part of it, for unpaid housework. Only five per cent of the women who were surveyed work only eight hours a day; 55 per cent of them work between eight and 12 hours; and 29 per cent work between 12 and 16 hours. After the change in the law, 73 per cent of women had to reduce one or more monthly expense.

The government had promised that after Law 789 was enacted, 160,000 new jobs would be created every year. However, the Superintendencia de Sociedades (a government body that inspects, supervises, and controls trading companies) reported that in 2003 only 5,923 new jobs had been generated. There is no data about subsequent years, but as the unemployment rate has not varied a great deal, one can conclude that Law 789 did not fulfil its stated goal.

Other campaigns tackled longer-standing problems. In Nicaragua, young women make up 85 per cent of the labour force in the *maquilas*. The absence of health and safety legislation – or the inadequate enforcement of the policies that do exist – are major problems. The campaign in Nicaragua focused on putting in place strong instruments that would promote respect for the health and safety of women workers, with the slogan 'Workplace health and safety…is my right!'

The campaign in Sri Lanka also focused on the wages and other conditions of women workers in factories. However, the campaign was initiated by the effect of the phase-out of the Multifibre Arrangement (MFA) on workers in the clothing industry in Sri Lanka (see Box 2).

Box 2: The end of quotas

Cheap exports of garments and textiles from low-cost producers in developing countries threaten garment producers in developed countries. For many years, the trade was governed by the Multifibre Arrangement (MFA). This imposed a quota system, which protected garment producers in the USA and European Union countries and provided many developing countries with access to those markets and shelter from the rigours of global competition. The Agreement on Textiles and Clothing (ATC) set out the process of phasing out the MFA .

On 1 January 2005 the ATC process came to an end. Developing countries which relied on their quota for textile exports now had to compete with the world's cheapest garment-producing countries, particularly with China. For clothing brands and retailers in importing countries, the constriction of quotas had meant paying higher prices (although unit costs have been getting cheaper) and also having to maintain complex supply chains to source from a large number of countries and suppliers. The ending of the ATC meant that they could consolidate their supply base to those countries and suppliers that offer the best deal in terms of price, quality, service, and turn-around time, and where the risks in terms of political instability, insecurity, and association with human-rights abuse are minimised.

The quota regime had enabled many developing countries to establish a garment industry, which has been a source of economic growth and foreign earnings, has created jobs, and has provided some workers with a steady income. However, many of these newly established industries were uncompetitive. Quotas allowed them to trade without taking the steps to build an efficient, competitive industry by, for example, developing modern infrastructure and communications. The end of quotas seriously affected these countries. For garment workers in vulnerable countries, and the organisations which represent them, the end of the MFA brings fears of large-scale job losses as well as downward pressure on working conditions. The International Monetary Fund estimates that the end of the quota regime will cost 19 million jobs in developing countries.[6]

32

In the USA, FLOC's collective bargaining agreements with cucumber growers in Ohio were being undermined by lower priced non-union cucumbers produced in North Carolina. The biggest buyer of cucumbers in North Carolina was Mt. Olive Packing Company, which purchased cucumbers from a large number of growers and processed them as pickles under its Mt. Olive brand. The buyers of cucumbers in Ohio threatened to move their operations to North Carolina, unless FLOC accepted lower wages. In response, FLOC sent organisers to North Carolina to organise the cucumber workers. Since many of the growers who produced cucumbers for Mt. Olive also belonged to the North Carolina Growers' Association (NCGA), both Mt. Olive and the NCGA became targets for FLOC's union campaign.

In this way, FLOC identified a particular group of workers whose rights were being violated: male Mexican migrant workers in the vegetable farms of North Carolina. Their situation was made more difficult by their circumstances. As immigrant workers, they were not covered by the National Labor Relations Act, the main law governing union organisation in the USA. As temporary, non-unionised workers from Mexico dispersed across hundreds of farms, they were susceptible to abuse by the growers. This dispersal, and the seasonal migration between Mexico and the USA, also created a problem for FLOC related to worker organisation drives (intense organising processes with the objective of finding a certain number people willing to be members of a formal organisation – most often a union).

Under section H2A of US immigration law, workers holding H2A visas (also known as 'guest workers') are allowed to enter the country to work for a specific employer, and must leave soon after the picking season ends. This means that guest workers depend on their employer both for their jobs and for the right to remain in the USA, so they are at the mercy of their employers and subject to exploitation and mistreatment. Representing guest workers is a lot more complicated than representing the average American union worker. First, communicating with guest workers is difficult, because they work in the USA on a seasonal basis, and at the end of the work period they return to Mexico, where they are hard to contact. Second, guest workers face unique problems as they navigate their way, each year, though the US immigration system to get to their jobs. Third, once they reach the USA they are isolated in remote agricultural areas with no means of transport, making it more difficult to build union solidarity and enforce their contract rights.

To complete the analysis under this heading, the problem identified in Morocco could be described as the government's reluctance or failure to enforce the provisions of its own labour code. Moroccan NGOs might presume or anticipate this reluctance or failure, based on their experience of the government's enforcement of regulations.

Building National Campaigns: Activists, Alliances, and How Change Happens

So far, we have discussed problems that were identified at the start of the campaign, but it is possible that problems will emerge once the campaign has started, to which the alliance will feel they can or should respond. The alliance in Colombia campaigned against a proposal to change women's retirement age which emerged in this way.

Defining a solution

Defining the problem often suggests the changes in policy and practice that will solve or improve it. Sometimes this is a solution that is winnable, or 'for now'; an intermediate step. Alliances often have to decide whether it is feasible to propose a solution or whether the context demands simply avoiding a setback. When a solution is proposed or achieved, new problems may need to be addressed. For some members of alliances, for instance in Morocco, this was their first experience of proposing solutions to address the causes of a structural problem (lack of labour-law enforcement, particularly in industrial sectors with a high percentage of women workers), rather than trying to influence a law-making process or protesting in response to specific events.

Given the scale and long-entrenched nature of labour-rights abuses, it is not surprising that solutions are often partial and continuing. It is also to be expected that FLOC, a trade union, saw union membership and recognition by the employers' association as the solution to the problems of migrant workers. Once this has been achieved, the workers can press for specific improvements in pay and working conditions through the union, with reasonable hope of success. The successful end-point of the campaign is the beginning of a long-term process of negotiating improvements, and continuing to recruit newly arrived workers to join the union.

FLOC's challenges do not end there. There are two forces pushing them backwards. One is that North Carolina is a 'right to work' state. This means that an employee under a union contract can refuse to pay union dues and still get the benefits of the contract. This presents a constant challenge for a union to maintain its membership, since employees can get a 'free ride' under right-to-work laws. Secondly, now that the North Carolina Growers' Association (NCGA) is under union contract, an anti-union employers' association has been formed to oppose the NCGA and fight unionisation in agriculture. This new organisation, called MAS H2A, started recruiting members in North Carolina in October 2005. MAS H2A wrote to every grower in the NCGA asking the grower to reject the FLOC/NCGA union contract by leaving NCGA and joining it instead. MAS H2A would recruit guest workers for its members but without a union contract. So far 18 employers have left the NCGA in response to this activity.

Similarly, in Morocco, the nature of the campaign implies a long-term process of enforcing the provisions of the labour code, accompanied by the trade unions researching and drawing attention to cases where the code is being breached. The alliance had a strategic discussion about whether the campaign should call for national labour legislation to reflect international conventions (this would require reforming the law that had just passed) or whether they should call for enforcement (because even if the law isn't in line with international conventions, it isn't being enforced). They concluded that if they wanted to start changing the reality on the ground they needed to work with what was available, and reform the law once they had made some progress.

Some members of the alliance in Nicaragua were involved in a larger effort in which they developed a legislative proposal on health and safety. At times, MEC in its own right has actively proposed new legislation to defend workers' rights. As they campaigned together, the whole alliance worked for the approval of the bill on health and safety (as we'll see below). Thus, they were experienced in several stages of working towards a solution. The alliance in Sri Lanka saw needs in the areas of employer and state responsibility respectively. The garment industry should pay a living wage to its workers, recognise their right to freedom of association, compensate workers who lost their jobs, and improve living conditions in migrant workers' hostels; and the government should help the industry which was badly affected by the phase-out of the MFA, and particularly workers who had lost their jobs.

Given the damaging nature of Law 789, the ultimate aim of the campaign in Colombia would be to repeal the law. However, the government in Colombia is so much on the side of the employers that the alliance had to work hard to prevent the passage of laws which would have further increased the disadvantages of working women. In these circumstances, the alliance had the interim goal of raising awareness of the consequences of Law 789, and hence opposition to the law.

Targets

Just as the problem often implies a solution, so the solution often implies the target – the institution, or sometimes the individual, with the power to change policy or practice, and hence the institution which the alliance must persuade, convince, or put pressure on.

FLOC had two closely linked targets. The North Carolina Growers' Association (NCGA) was the association of growers who directly employed the migrant farm workers. NCGA organised the hiring of workers for the growers. Mt. Olive was a food company which processed, packaged, and sold pickles made from crops it bought from members of the NCGA. The initial idea was that the growers in North Carolina would be the opponent, but after further analysis FLOC realised that the big opponent was Mt. Olive because they were 'price placers'. Since Mt. Olive sold its products to consumers, it was vulnerable to the pressure of a consumer boycott, and would, in turn, put pressure on NCGA. FLOC also had to deal directly with NCGA because they were the employers of the workers FLOC wanted to unionise. It is interesting that FLOC did not target the government, although there is legislation dealing with payment of wages and governing the working conditions of H2A workers. The union felt that government regulation of farm labour was ineffective, slow, and unsatisfactory, but rather than try to improve those laws, it concentrated on the more achievable aim of influencing Mt. Olive and NCGA. However, alone among the case studies discussed here, FLOC made use of the courts. It brought a 'class action lawsuit' (by which a small number of claims holders are allowed under US civil law to represent all others with similar legal claims) for violations of state and federal wage laws against the NCGA, to add to the pressure from other sources.

All the other alliances targeted their national government in one way or another – to legislate, to enforce legislation, to support industry, or a combination of these actions. The detail determines the precise target. In Morocco, the targets were government and local employers (according to the alliance's power analysis, both contribute to weak labour-law enforcement). Because the alliance chose to focus on implementation of the law, they targeted the relevant minister and his officials. Internal debates within the Moroccan alliance are illuminating about the other potential targets. One option is to target members of the country's parliament. Some people in the alliance believe that members of parliament can add to the campaign's leverage through their profile, by inviting the alliance to debates, and advocating for the rights of women workers in parliament. Others argue that members of parliament would not add anything substantial as individuals, but a parliamentary group could be a significant political support as this 'would be more official'. A second potential target is the employers. At present the alliance does not feel ready to sit with the employers at the same table. Some believe, however, that a round-table discussion on labour-law enforcement or corporate social responsibility could potentially be an important step.

The alliance in Sri Lanka targeted employers, the government, buyers, and some international actors (such as the European Union, among others). As we will see later, the alliance worked with the Department of Labour on a survey of all garment-manufacturing factories in Sri Lanka. The alliance also prompted the International Labour Organisation (ILO) through their local office to convene a task force comprising employers, trade unions, NGOs, and government departments – as well as ALaRM itself, to develop a strategy to deal with the job losses that were envisaged in the apparel sector due to the MFA phase-out.

In Nicaragua, the alliance sought improvements to the law, so they targeted the legislature – and MEC also targeted the president, who has a constitutional role in introducing legislative proposals. In Colombia, many allies initially expected more support from the government or particular politicians, especially when discussing the issue from the perspective of women's rights. The alliance targeted individual members of congress, aiming to make them 'collaborators' with the alliance. After elections to congress in March 2006, the alliance vigorously approached new women members to make them aware of the issue of women's labour rights. They also made contact with presidential candidates to make them aware of the importance of women's labour rights. The advantage of this tactic is that if all the presidential candidates promise action, then the lobbying process after the election has a very favourable start.

It should be noted that all the alliances were able to lobby their chosen targets – they operated in a political environment which allowed space for organisations to exist, to make demands, and to mobilise workers and the wider public. The alliances created space by attaining a certain degree of legitimacy, either from the strength of their particular alliance, or through a particular alliance member, or due to the amount of media coverage they obtained. The space didn't automatically exist in any country – it was pried open. Even in Colombia, where there has been 30 years of civil war and there are hundreds of politically motivated assassinations every year, organisations are able to function and mobilise large numbers of people.

Audiences

All the alliances sought support for their campaigns from the wider public, opinion-makers in the media, and workers in the relevant industries. The reasons to address certain audiences varied. It is important that alliances define the audience and clarify and agree on the reasons to target that audience: what change is expected? How will this further the aims of the campaign?

It is important to inform the public about all aspects of the campaign: the issue, the problem, the proposed solution, and the alliance carrying out the campaign. Public awareness of the issue and support for the campaign provide a favourable background for everything the alliance may try to do, influencing politicians, employers, the media, and the workers. When there is sufficient public interest and concern, it is possible to mobilise the public to take action, as a later section will describe. Most importantly, public support will help sustain any achievements over the long run. The most effective way to reach the public is through the media. In Colombia, the campaign has developed a good media strategy in order to create a good public environment. If public opinion shows that most of the people are supporting the campaign's points of view, congress and the government may feel that they have at least to listen to the argument of the campaign. For each event the alliance selected the messages (according to the event and the political context), and the targets (congress, government, etc.) Public opinion is key in Colombia, because of the stigmatisation of and violence against trade-union leaders.

There is a fuller discussion of media work below, but at this stage we should note the distinction between reporting and commentary. The campaign wants the news media to report on the activities and views of the alliance; and also wants individuals in the media of entertainment and opinion to lend their support to the campaign. Prestigious commentators in the serious press will influence organisations, employers, and the government; celebrities from the world of entertainment will influence the wider public. The campaign in Colombia provides examples of both these tactics (see Box 3).

Box 3: Support from opinion leaders and celebrities

Rudolf Homes is a former minister of the treasury, a former dean of the Universidad de los Andes (the most important private university in Colombia), a well-known defender of neo-liberalism, and one of the most widely read columnists of the only national newspaper, *El Tiempo*. In one of his columns, he questioned a senator on comments she had made in opposition to the free trade agreement between Colombia and the USA. Homes argued that with the agreement 'women will have employment and they won't be seen begging in the streets'. For him, a bad job was better than none at all. The alliance had kept up constant monitoring of the columns written by opinion leaders and was prepared to send a letter in reply. The alliance's letter focused its arguments on the fundamental and inalienable right of women to a decent job, and the importance of it as a strategy to end poverty and discrimination. Homes used these arguments in his following columns, acknowledged the

alliance's campaign, questioned the business community and the government about the validity of the arguments, and asked them to give an answer to the alliance members. The airing of these issues in Homes' columns was very important, as many people read them.

The alliance was equally effective at recruiting celebrities. People in member organisations used their social and family networks to make first contact, and persuaded female celebrities to show solidarity with women workers. The celebrities included a well-known and respected

Two Colombian folk music celebrities, Petrona Martínez and Etelvina Maldonado, sing and entertain at the International Women's Day celebrations, 8 March 2005.
Source: MTF – My Rights are Not Negotiable

This is the Columbia campaign t-shirt which in 2007 is still in use. The logo reads: 'Make trade fair – my rights are not negotiable'.
Source: MTF – My Rights are Not Negotiable

historian, a poet, and a dancer, and many of them were singers (folklore and rock groups). The very different array of public figures allowed the alliance to reach out to very different audiences. So many singers supported the campaign that it was possible to put on a concert, and record a CD, 'Women's voices', which has been distributed free of charge at various events. As an alliance member said:

'The CD is part of our new communication items highly valued by those who have access to it. It has become one of our best introductions to present the campaign.'

Perhaps most encouraging for the alliance was that another celebrity, a popular star of Colombian cinema and television, gave her support spontaneously. She had seen a woman wearing the campaign t-shirt and, of her own volition, she contacted the co-ordinators to let them know that she wanted to give her support. Her joining the campaign still causes favourable comments from the wider public. She was received with joy within the alliance because they felt that her participation was proof that the alliance's message was good, and was reaching out widely.

Workers will, of course, see and hear messages aimed at the wider public. But all the alliances also communicated directly with workers in the relevant industry. They are a key audience for several reasons. Any policy or practice change will need to be reinforced daily by workers claiming their rights in the workplace. Since the campaign is for their ultimate benefit, it is appropriate that they should know about it. Their views, problems, and information should feed into the analysis underlying the campaign. Workers' testimonies and case studies provide valuable reinforcement to the more generalised messages directed at the target institutions and the media. Workers' voices are the change already. In the context of a long-term campaign on big issues, it is good to achieve small, tangible successes by informing workers about their rights – both for the immediate benefit of the workers themselves, and as a reassurance to the members of the alliance and to the wider world that campaigning can work.

Some women workers are campaign activists. Other women workers form the audience for the campaign's message. They are not necessarily passive – some of them may become activists as a result of the campaign. When women move on to become activists, they become protagonists of their own rights, embodying the change itself. They tell their own stories rather than being spoken about. In many countries it is dangerous for women workers to speak out, because of the political situation and social and gender inequality. This danger means that it is even more significant when women workers do speak out and become active.

There are several audiences for women workers' campaign messages. One audience is the decision-makers, and for them the message is about change in policy and practice. Another audience is the wider society, and for this audience the message is about the value of women's work. This helps to create a climate of opinion which will encourage decision-makers to be open to policy change. Yet another audience is the women workers themselves, and for them the message is to monitor the implementation of policy change. To sum up, campaigning can change opinion in the wider society. Helped by this changed climate of opinion, campaigning can persuade decision-makers to change policies. Campaigning can then make women workers aware of the policy change, so they monitor whether it is implemented in their place of work. And campaigning with women workers can encourage some of them to become campaign activists.

All of these points are true of all the alliances, but the FLOC campaign merits a special mention. It was essential to the success of the boycott that as many people as possible heard of and supported the campaign. Rather than public opinion backing up other campaign actions, the effort to influence public opinion and invite them to action was a key campaign strategy. Similarly, communication with the relevant workers was not just useful in all the ways mentioned immediately above, but essential to prepare the ground for the urgent sign-up drive once agreement had been reached with the NCGA. FLOC could not rely on messages in US media reaching workers, because they would be in English rather than Spanish; so FLOC ensured that they communicated directly with the workers in Spanish.

Actions

We now come to the core of the campaign strategy. The range of actions is large, and for clarity of presentation will be organised into three main categories: lobbying, mobilisation, and training. In practice, most alliances did all three, and they are mutually supportive and complementary.

Lobbying

Lobbying can consist of private appeals to officials and decision-makers, public actions (for example mass demonstrations), or combinations of both public and private actions (for example, encouraging constituents to contact their government representatives). Lobbying can be very effective when the approach is co-operative rather than confrontational. The alliance can convince the government by providing information, alerting it to problems, suggesting legislation, or monitoring implementation.

Many alliances put the case for changes in government policy or practice directly to the relevant government department or minister. In Morocco the alliance wrote to the minister of employment in March 2005, and the minister agreed to meet the alliance in May 2005. Several factors may have helped to get this meeting: that the country's two largest unions were part of the alliance; that the letter was accompanied by a brochure setting out the alliance's position, which gave the alliance a more professional image and presented a common platform; and that the brochure was supported by an international actor (Oxfam). The timing was also good, as we will see in a later section.

The alliance prepared carefully for the meeting. They drew up an agenda covering the topics to be discussed and the order in which the alliance members would speak. Preparation is important because it helps give a professional image, cohesion to the group and to the argument to be presented, and avoids disagreements between members in front of the government, or after the meeting. The alliance held a strategic discussion before the meeting to prioritise the demands that had been agreed in the brochure. There was a recognition that the alliance could not ask for everything at once and had to identify a few priority points to discuss with the minister at this first meeting. Members agreed that demands they made had to be achievable and concrete so that the minister could give specific responses. This also helped allies to follow up on his words and commitments later.

The meeting was considered a success by the allies, in the sense that they managed to start a dialogue with the government. The minister appointed the employment director as the alliance's interlocutor to follow up on this dialogue in the future. The alliance sent the minister a thank-you letter, and wrote to the employment director informing him of the minister's action and requesting a follow-up meeting. The meeting was arranged in September 2005. Terms of reference for the meeting (including objective, roles, and key messages) were drawn up by the campaign co-ordinator, and discussed and agreed by alliance members. In the months following the meeting, the alliance monitored the points presented by the employment director and sought information about their implementation. This was done in order to have more concrete recommendations and examples so as to hold the government to account at the next meeting. Some members found that this meeting was more important than the one with the minister because the discussion was more focused on policy points and because the meeting was followed up (the director invited the alliance to a couple of seminars). A second meeting with the director is also under preparation.

The alliance in Nicaragua had as one of its campaign objectives the passing of a National Occupational Health and Safety Law. Rather than lobby the legislature to write a bill, the alliance wrote and presented the bill (through the Ministry of Labour) to the National Assembly. It has not yet been approved. MEC also presented to the president's office a proposal for a national employment policy with a focus on gender equality, which was subsequently approved. The speed of its approval was seen as a response to the legitimacy of MEC and the campaign work.

In Colombia, congress debated pension reform. There was a proposal that as women live longer than men, women's retirement age should be increased. The alliance lobbied individual women members of congress, and succeeded in getting the proposal dropped. However, the issue is under consideration again after recent recommendations by the World Bank, so the alliance is once again putting the counter-argument, especially to the recently elected women members of congress mentioned earlier.

The Colombia campaign opposes Law 789, and at the same time presses for consistency in its application. Before the law was passed, politicians promoted it by saying it would create jobs. They promised to prove this by creating a commission to review its impact. They made the requirement to establish the commission a part of the law. However, they have not yet created the commission. The campaign alliance has gathered evidence to show that in fact the law has not generated more jobs. They want to present the evidence to the commission. So they are demanding that the government respects the law and implements it, by establishing the commission.

In Sri Lanka, the MFA task force realised that there should be accurate data about the apparel industry in order to decide on strategies and interventions to address the impact of the MFA phase-out on the workers. The Department of Labour had the capacity to do a survey and gather all the details because they had a country-wide network of offices. ALaRM offered to provide the required technical and financial assistance. So the alliance and the Department of Labour together did a national survey of all garment factories in October 2004, gathering much-needed accurate data which had not previously existed. It is important to see where it is possible to use existing resources in this way.

In the initiative with the ILO described earlier, the alliance in Sri Lanka took the approach of co-operating with the employers. At other times, they opposed the employers, in particular when calling on them not to postpone a planned increase in wages for workers in the industry. Alliance members also became involved in local efforts to help workers access funds intended for them. It is useful to work with employers when you can, but important to maintain independence.

In most countries, campaigners dealing with the government can plausibly claim a shared interest in the well-being of the people. However, the story changes when it comes to employers, and most of the campaigns have met resistance from this quarter. FLOC, in the USA, could not disguise that its objectives ran counter to those of the NCGA. Growers wanted to pay their workers as little as they could, and to prevent the unionisation of their workforce which would be likely to help the workers to increase their wages and improve working conditions. In negotiations between FLOC and NCGA, a win for FLOC would be seen as a loss by NCGA. Indeed, it took great pressure to force NCGA to the negotiating table. Some of that pressure came from mobilisation, as described below, but it also included a class action lawsuit against NCGA for violations of minimum wage laws, which later resulted in a $12m judgement.

However, in parallel with this confrontational stance, FLOC organisers in the labour camps set up negotiations between workers and employers over small and uncontroversial issues. (This tactic echoes the importance of finding small and uncontroversial areas of agreement between members of the alliance, as part of the alliance-building process.) For instance, workers in one camp asked for a supply of water during the working day. (The right to have water to drink meets such a fundamental need that it should not be described as 'small' – but the point here is that it is uncontroversial and easy for the employer to supply.) As one worker said 'there's nothing wrong with asking, and we're not complaining'. As a result, employers gained respect for FLOC organisers.

Once the main objectives of unionisation and recognition had been achieved, the two sides entered into a more co-operative way of working. FLOC reached agreement with NCGA to allow it to oversee the process of employing over 8,000 workers from across Mexico who work in North Carolina. FLOC and the NCGA recently reached a settlement in the $12m class action lawsuit judgement (which had threatened to bankrupt the NCGA). FLOC agreed to lower its damages award in exchange for an agreement by the NCGA to give preference in hiring to union employees and to pay the transportation and H2A visa fees for employees.

Mobilisation

Lobbying usually involves small numbers of people, often literally sitting around a table. Mobilisation involves large numbers of people showing support for a campaign. Actions are carefully chosen, because they require lots of time and resources. Even when the campaign strategy does not involve mobilising supporters, it is helpful for the campaigning organisations, and the institutions they are negotiating with, to know that they have supporters. Some mobilisation is intended primarily to influence a decision-maker, some to build awareness and organisation among the participants. It could be argued that the alliance in Morocco gained access to the minister because he knew that they had large numbers of members. This gave them legitimacy, and carried the implicit threat that if he did not talk to the members of the alliance, they could mobilise their members to put pressure on him.

Hundreds of FLOC supporters march through the town of Mt. Olive in the USA, supporting the pickle boycott during a major demonstration (2003). Farm-worker activists help bystanders make the link between poor factory conditions and 'sweatshops without walls' in the fields.
Source: Joseph Brymer Photography

FLOC's campaign strategy included several forms of mobilisation. The consumer boycott, already mentioned above, needed the widest possible support to be effective. The boycott was supported by an extensive network that was reactivated and built up over the course of the campaign. The number of supporting organisations reached close to 250 and included a broad array of organisations, based in several states, representing varied interests ranging from labour, communications, churches of different denominations as well as interfaith groups, women's organisations, environmental groups, human-rights organisations, local community groups, student groups, local branches of political parties, service organisations, and immigrants' rights groups. Three major supermarket chains removed the pickles from their shelves and other chains considered doing so. FLOC used the media to reach the wider public, and also worked with students' groups and the Latino community; but the most important mobilisation in support of the boycott was through churches. Many of the local and state churches were doing some work around farm-worker issues, but no one connected them until FLOC came along. With the help of old allies, FLOC began mapping out and meeting with numerous progressive church congregations. An important component of the church work was that it was largely carried out by non-Latino staff and volunteers who had a closer cultural affinity with church members. FLOC organisers and volunteers used a variety of methods and resources to mobilise churches, some of which are described in Box 4.

FLOC also mobilised the support of the local community in Dudley, North Carolina. Community members provided such things as critical information about worker needs and the employers' situation, volunteers, donations of food, money, and other necessities, protection for workers, housing, new staff, entertainment and cultural connections to FLOC staff and to workers, and a support base for workers and organisers. The most direct and crucial connection between FLOC and the community was through Angelita Morrisroe and her grocery store, *La Palmita*, as described earlier.

At the same time, FLOC mobilised the workers. Good contacts with the workers helped with the mobilisation of churches, by facilitating testimonies and visits as described in Box 4. Small meetings built up trust between the workers and FLOC organisers, and identified achievable goals for local negotiations with employers, as discussed above. FLOC also provided services to the workers, including translation, transportation to health clinics, English classes, and help with form-filling, as a means of building trust between workers and the union. Workers began to lose their sense of isolation and fear of the employers, and to have understanding and confidence in what they could achieve collectively. FLOC staff made frequent use of cell (mobile) phones, which many workers had. FLOC organisers also gave out cell-phone and home numbers and addresses to workers and made themselves available to them as needed. The organisers were prepared to go where the workers were, and this included farms all over North Carolina,

Box 4: Mobilising churches in the Mt. Olive campaign

FLOC developed and distributed 'Pickle Picket Packets' – a 'do-it-yourself' kit for awareness raising and organising a church. They contained guides illustrating how to do such things as co-ordinate a church campaign, how to approach church members and shoppers, how to deal with the police and the media, and how to develop posters and banners. The packet also included songs and other materials aiding the process of establishing individual farm-worker committees in churches.

The Church of Reconciliation (USA) organises a picket at a local grocery store in 2002, pressurising it to stop selling pickles in support of the Mt. Olive pickle boycott.
Source: Lori Fernald Khamala

Organisers and committed church members included workers in the campaign by inviting them to congregations to give testimonies of their experience. Testimonies put a human face on the campaign and presented real-life experiences to congregations. Church members met people with whom they would not usually come into contact. The organisers encouraged them to write to clergy, politicians, supermarkets, and Mt. Olive officials to express their concern about farm-worker issues. They were also encouraged to recruit other church members, family members, and community members. FLOC invited church members to visit labour camps, to meet and interact with farm workers. This served multiple purposes including reinforcing the commitment of the church members, building relationships and communication between them and workers, and providing workers with a connection to the larger community.

FLOC also worked with local-level activists within churches, to take the campaign up to the national-level church organisations such as the United Church of Christ, United Council of Churches, and United Methodist Church (UMC). An unplanned breakthrough moment came when the world body of the UMC met in the USA. FLOC (which had been unsuccessful in gaining support for its boycott from the American UMC up to that moment) capitalised on this opportunity to lobby for support from UMC delegates from developing countries, who pushed through a resolution in support of the boycott. The Chief Executive of Mt. Olive, Bill Bryan, was a respected UMC member who promoted his company as a 'Christian business with local, small town values'. The combination of the local, national, and international campaigns made a powerful impact on the devout leader of the company and on its image. In the words of a FLOC organiser, 'The UMC was a key battle site'.

All this mobilisation was done through so-called 'progressive' churches, with which FLOC had an established relationship. But FLOC also worked successfully with conservative evangelical churches. Among the tactics used by FLOC to gain evangelical support was to relate the Bible's teaching on social justice to the injustices suffered by the immigrant workers 'here and now'.

as well as Florida and Mexico – the places the workers returned to after the season for farm work was over.

Perhaps the most significant benefit of this preliminary mobilisation among the workers was to pave the way for the sign-up campaign. Once FLOC had persuaded NCGA to agree to allow workers to exercise their right to organise, the union had 30 days to sign up workers and show that a majority wanted to join. The organisers had to get sign-up initially from 10,500 workers scattered across more than 1000 farms spread over 60 counties in North Carolina. FLOC called on allies including university students and the AFL-CIO to add to its own organisers and volunteers. Their job was made possible by the relationship of trust that FLOC had built up with the workers in the earlier phase of the campaign. The success of the sign-up campaign cemented the success of the boycott campaign and the negotiations with NCGA and Mt. Olive.

The other three alliances also used the tactic of getting signatures. The Sri Lanka alliance organised a workers' petition in support of the demand not to delay a planned pay increase in the garment industry. As with all petitions, it was essential that people should know what they were signing for. The alliance produced a leaflet explaining the demands, and organisers distributed the leaflet and gathered signatures.

In Colombia, the alliance gained 15,000 signatures backing the campaign against Law 789, and supporting a global petition ('Big Noise') to Make Trade Fair, as part of the campaign of the same name. They distributed cards which set out the alliance's position, so that people would know what they were signing. Another form of mobilisation was to organise a major celebration to mark International Women's Day. Similarly, the alliance in Sri Lanka encouraged women workers to celebrate May Day (the first of May is an internationally recognised day of celebration for organised labour).

International Women's Day, Colombia 2005.
Some people are standing on stilts to attract public attention and support.
Source: MTF – My Rights are Not Negotiable

The alliance in Nicaragua mobilised workers and the general public in support of the lobbying actions already described above. Women workers from the *maquilas* collected 11,160 signatures in support of the bill presented to the National Assembly. Under Nicaraguan law, any legally established organisation can present a proposal for law if it gathers at least 5,000 signatures. In support of the proposal to the president's office, the alliance organised two national conferences, each with 1,500 women workers as well as the president, other government ministers, and business leaders.

Training

Many alliances included training for workers in their campaign strategy, and some felt the need for training for their own members.

If the campaign's objective is to organise and/or mobilise workers, training workers about their rights and other issues is worthwhile in that it brings immediate benefits to the workers if they gain the knowledge and confidence to defend their own rights. Any policy change needs to be enforced by workers claiming their rights every day. Training also creates trust between workers and alliance members, helps the alliance find out useful information, and prepares the ground for action and mobilisation. Alliance members may identify participants in training as potential volunteer organisers.

The Colombia alliance organised a 'training tour' which reached out from the capital, Bogotá, to four other cities: Medellín, Cali, Cartagena, and Barranquilla. About 150 women attended the workshops where they discussed women's labour rights, the impact of Law 789, and the consequences of the proposed free trade agreement with the USA. In these workshops they also collected case-study information about the impact of Law 789 on real women's lives. Alliance leaders used these regional workshops to recruit locally based organisations to the alliance, giving the campaign an active presence in cities across the country. This, in turn, will have benefits in terms of mobilisation and potentially lobbying congress members from those cities.

In Nicaragua the training for women workers in the *maquilas* was relatively comprehensive and systematic. It covered personal and domestic themes as well as occupational issues, touching on self-esteem, gender equality, sexual and reproductive health, family planning, safety risks and prevention in the workplace, workplace accidents, occupational illness, and infectious diseases, among other topics. MEC's approach is that women learn and understand their rights in all of their lives, not just in the workplace. The training was reinforced by the use of publications and distribution of support materials about labour rights, the free trade agreement between the USA, Central America, and the Dominican Republic, and sexual and reproductive health, among other topics. These materials were distributed to women workers from different factories. Specialists from the organisations in the Network – the Health Ministry, the Pan American Health Organization, the National Autonomous University of Nicaragua, the Nicaraguan Institute of Social Security (INSS), and the Labour Ministry – formed part of the training team that worked throughout the campaign. In the case of the ministries, the trainers were people involved in resolving workers' problems as part of their daily jobs, and the workshops allowed them the opportunity to hear directly from the workers in their own words.

The campaign in Sri Lanka aimed to help the workers to see themselves as part of a bigger system where there are other actors allied with them, and to give them a sense of their effectiveness that they may not have had before. The alliance trained workers on the content of labour law, how to monitor labour rights, and workplace health and safety, and workers were able to apply the new skills they had learnt. In many cases, workers had been afraid to mobilise and demonstrate for fear of retribution, including being fired. As a result of training they became more confident that the institutional backing they had, both locally and internationally, would provide them with some measure of protection. This training was organised by the partner organisations.

FLOC's dialogue with the workers in North Carolina included informing them about action taken by other workers in different places, suggesting options for action, and providing information about the legal system and government agencies. While this was tied to particular local issues, and informal compared with other examples, it could still be described as training. FLOC used cartoons, theatre, music, slide shows, and videos, all in Spanish, to get information across to the workers. FLOC's work with churches, described in Box 4 above, also included an element of training in campaigning techniques which many church congregations might not have encountered before.

In Morocco, Oxfam provided advocacy training to the other members of the alliance. This was intended to help the alliance to plan a comprehensive campaign in all its dimensions (lobby, media, research, mobilisation, etc.). The training was considered an important stage by some members, because it was a joint brainstorming exercise that brought members together and helped them to conceptualise a campaign strategy and policy objectives. It was particularly helpful in making some members understand the value of rigorous preparation and follow-up of meetings with the government, which were to form such an important part of the campaign strategy.

All the members of the alliance in Sri Lanka benefited from a training workshop organised by Oxfam, and from regular learning sessions on diverse technical topics which gave much-needed and most up-to-date information. Oxfam also attempted to ensure that all ALaRM member organisations were invited to workshops and seminars conducted by other organisations on related topics, thus providing them with the maximum possible opportunities to learn and expand their knowledge base.

The alliance in Colombia organised media training for women 'who have not had the chance to speak in public, whose audience is limited to the four walls of their house'. To be able to stand in front of a camera, make statements on the radio, or answer questions for a newspaper interview are all skills, and without them the experience can be unnerving and the message may not get across clearly. Thanks to the training, aimed at strengthening the abilities of women to be spokespeople, 'new voices came out, voices with grace and warmth, voices with a distinct language talking about globalisation and social inequality'.

Who does what?

In relatively fragile, recently established alliances, such as that in Morocco, it is important that all the members are equally involved, and that no member does conspicuously more, or less, than the others. Members usually dedicated between half a day and two days per month on average to work for the alliance. For others, working for the alliance overlapped with their own work. More long-established alliances can be more relaxed, and allocate work as appropriate. In the USA, FLOC allocated actions to allies in a way that could almost be described as delegation.

In Nicaragua, the executive committee co-ordinated the work to enable every member of the alliance to develop key actions to improve its work on labour and health rights. The labour ministry centred its commitments on inspections of the special zones with the aim of verifying compliance with health and safety regulations. The Nicaraguan Institute for Social Security (INSS) made a commitment to investigate the origin of the most frequent illnesses in order to recommend changes in the working environment; and to supervise compliance with the legal responsibilities for social security by employers. The Pan American Health Organization made a commitment to continue its work in training businesses and workers from different sectors in the methodology known as Tool Box, aimed at promoting healthy environments in factories.

The alliance in Colombia agreed that specific tasks should be carried out by the organisations with the most relevant experience. For instance, relations with congress were developed by the representatives of two NGOs whose work is precisely to lobby within the legislative arena. Women's organisations with experience of training processes for women have been responsible for capacity-building, and organisations with research experience are responsible for producing documents. At the local level there is the same division of labour.

It is important that who does what is formally decided and the decision recorded and shared with everyone. Oxfam's role developed as the campaigns moved forward, and for that reason, the role varied and was different according to every situation. That is the key lesson for any supporting agency.

Timing

The problems of precariously employed workers, and the numbers affected, are so great that action is required urgently and it is regrettable if there is any delay in solving the problems. On the other hand, the organisations making up the campaigning alliances have many other demands on their time and resources and it is unrealistic to expect instant action, let alone instant success. Furthermore, effective action needs good preparation. Patient preparation with the workers enabled FLOC to make the most of the sign-up opportunity when it came.

The Nicaraguan alliance gathered information and views from women workers to feed into its proposed legislation.

Even so, some members of the Moroccan alliance felt that work at government level had taken place too quickly, before building a base on the ground. They felt that the alliance should now mobilise to support and involve women workers and organise an awareness-raising campaign:

'Six people, a small alliance, cannot do much if they are not directly connected to the target group in question. We cannot put pressure on the government if our campaign is not reflected in a population group and is not supported by this group, and even better by the public. We should establish a direct relationship with the women workers, and work together with them. We should…organise actions that support women workers in case of violations of their rights'.

Another reason to take action at one time rather than another is to take advantage of an opportunity provided by a given date. In Sri Lanka, as in many countries, May Day is a day of celebration for organised labour. However, because the majority of the workers in the garment sector are not unionised, they cannot participate in traditional May Day celebrations that are organised by the trade unions. The members of ALaRM decided to celebrate May Day differently. They organised a procession with music and a cultural feel, instead of the traditional, aggressive marches and slogans. This reduced non-unionised workers' fear of participation in a May Day rally.

The alliance in Colombia chose to organise a big event on 8 March, International Women's Day. There was a march with flags waving and shouted slogans, and when the crowd gathered in a city square they heard speeches from women representatives of the organisations in the alliance. (This event was also significant for the leaders of the alliance as a test of gender relations within the alliance, to be discussed below.) Less dramatically, at a different moment, the alliance took advantage of the fact that the main streets of Bogotá are closed to traffic on Sundays, to hand out campaign cards and collect signatures. In half a day they collected over 1,200 signatures.

This poster was held up by 'human statues' during a campaign stunt in Bogotá (Colombia) that took advantage of Sunday cycle days, when roads are closed to traffic. The white or gold painted statues would try to encourage people to sign up to request congress to review the impact of the labour-legislation reform on women. After passers-by signed a postcard and dropped it in their box, the statues would shake their hand.
Source: MTF – My Rights are Not Negotiable

In Morocco, when the alliance made their first approach to the minister they asked for a meeting date which fell about three weeks before May Day. They knew that the minister would be more open to talking to trade unions and broader civil society at around that time. May Day is recognised as a celebration for organised workers. In many countries in the world, government authorities frequently seek opportunities to at least appear to be 'in discussions' with workers' organisations, to neutralise any criticisms that might be directed at their work by those same workers' organisations.

As we have seen, FLOC provided help to workers in the labour camps and built up trust while working on a longer-term boycott campaign. They did not hesitate to organise and negotiate small achievable local actions; workers could benefit from small improvements in their conditions, pending the big improvement that they hoped would come with the achievement of unionisation.

While planning should take into account the necessary sequences of events, and make the most of known opportunities, there should also be a degree of flexibility to make the most of unexpected opportunities which may arise.

This applies particularly to media work, as discussed later. Equally, campaigners must be ready to respond to challenges as they arise. A good example pointed out earlier is the threat to increase women's retirement age in Colombia, which the alliance had to lobby against – and where they met with initial success.

All the alliances recognised the need for flexibility. Only MEC, in Nicaragua, wrote a formal detailed strategy. Other alliances had rolling strategies, identifying opportunities, and fuelled by progress (internally within the alliance or externally related to the issue – targets, media coverage, etc.). Even MEC, having started out with a strategy document, updated their strategy plans (though not always the document) on a rolling basis. In Colombia, this flexibility opened opportunities to work together with other alliances at key moments, which helped the visibility and reach of their own alliance.

Summary

To campaign effectively, it is essential to have a strategy. Otherwise the alliance will risk simply reacting to events, and taking actions which are not the best use of their scarce time and resources. A strategy should answer several related questions: what is the problem; what is our preferred solution; what can we actually win by working together; who has the power to deliver that solution; what are our targets and audiences; what action should we take, by whom, and when? The answers will, in turn, differ from place to place, depending on the country's political culture; the strengths and experience of the members in each alliance; and the campaigning issue. In addition to identifying and denouncing the problem, suggest realistic, feasible alternatives. A careful planning process should also keep asking the question 'why?'. It is easy for each member of the alliance to suggest actions with which it is familiar and comfortable. Strategic discussions should test these assumptions, and look for the best, most effective, action. Even well-established organisations can learn, improve, and innovate in the mutually supportive setting of a campaign alliance. Successful campaigns are unlikely to rely on only one type of action; typically, lobbying and mobilisation complement one another, and as we will see, all the campaigns included media work as well.

Key points

- Include in your strategy a vision of where you want to be when you have achieved your goals.

- Be aware of change in the external environment that may create unanticipated opportunities or unforeseen obstacles.

- Choose strategies that, if possible and appropriate, will also build people's capacity.

- Energise your campaign by moving beyond analysis and the 'perfect' solution to concrete actions and goals that are winnable. Invest time in understanding the institutional limits of your allies; it will save time and frustration later on.

- Review the organisations' capacity (skills and resources) that can be accessed during the period of time that the campaign will be running. In this way you will avoid choosing the best strategy without the means to implement it.

- Develop a strategy at the beginning of a campaign in order to teach alliance members early on about the importance of rigorous preparation and follow-up.

- Though most alliances struggle to ensure democratic functioning, remember to allocate work tasks appropriately, balancing relevant experience with the need to promote skills-development across all members.

- Make sure that the strategy includes follow-up work so that the alliance can corroborate that campaign achievements actually translate into concrete change on the ground.

4 • Incorporating gender equality

Overview

Women experience a wide range of disadvantages in almost every country in the world. These inequalities are manifested and reinforced both in workplaces and in employment arrangements. One of the consequences of inequality is that women make up the majority of workers in 'precarious' employment (see the Introduction for an explanation of this term).

In addition, women are vulnerable to sexual harassment at work, even violence in the workplace. And they find little understanding of their need to balance work and the demands of caring for their families.

In these circumstances, it is no surprise that four out of the five case-study campaigns focused on labour rights for women workers. All the alliances recognised the importance of incorporating gender equality not just in the aims of the campaign, but in the way it was carried out. The analysis in this chapter is, inevitably, generalised, and may be seen to stereotype men and women. To be clear – this analysis should not be taken to mean that all men (nor all women) are alike.

Women and men: changing power relations

Gender awareness goes beyond 'women's rights' or 'women's issues': it focuses on the power relationship between women and men. Some 'women's issues' are connected to their sex: rape, sexual harassment, reproductive health, and maternity leave. But other issues are connected to their position of subjection, suppression, or oppression by other social forces. Women suffer domestic violence (and violence in the workplace) from men, they receive lower wages than men, they do all or most of the household and child-care work because these roles are socially assigned to them rather than shared with men. A campaign that highlights gender inequality and intends to have a positive impact on the power relations between women and men requires attention to be paid to these issues at every stage.

Just because a campaign concerns women's rights at work, it does not necessarily mean that it addresses gender inequality. Campaigners may be working with women to solve their concrete problems, but not tackling the unequal power relationship which underlies those problems. Another way to put this is to contrast two possible descriptions of the issues behind a campaign on women's labour rights. On the one hand, it could be a campaign about labour rights in an industry where the majority of workers happen to be women, so women are presumed to benefit. On the other hand, it could be a campaign about valuing women's rights and challenging gender inequality, through a campaign about women's labour rights.

The challenge of many campaigns is to start with an analysis of the problem that campaigners want to work on and look at it in the light of gender inequality. The terms of reference for any research have to include questions about power relations between women and men. Often this requires finding new information that is collected and broken down by sex, rather than assuming that all workers, or all poor households have the same experience. This can be difficult in circumstances where a lot of the information often isn't available in gendered categories of analysis. Then participants must gather good anecdotal evidence and stories which highlight the issues that women face because of gender inequality, as well as other causes. It is crucial to make sure that the reports reflect this material, as sometimes, in the process of editing, these stories and data are minimised.

Likewise, strategies (campaigns, communications, etc.) must continue to highlight the gender-inequality issues in images, ways of working, messages, etc. The policy proposals must include mechanisms and actions to reduce inequality in power relations, rather than assuming that an overall proposal about workers will result in benefits for women workers. For example, women workers are found in higher percentages in informal employment, where labour legislation doesn't cover them, or where they cannot claim their rights because they cannot prove their status as a worker. Proposals about workers do not necessarily consider this distinction. Some proposals may not take into account existing discrimination. For example, if a minimum-wage proposal is based on a percentage and not an outright monetary figure, women workers who are facing salary discrimination may receive an increase in their wage with the proposal but will not have improved the salary discrimination situation at all.

The popular communications, where everything has to be communicated effectively (most often in short phrases) to a very broad audience, must echo the need to change the common myths and stereotypes that often reinforce the marginalisation of women.

It is important to portray women not as victims but as active, workers, and protagonists. For example, the Oxfam International Labour Rights Team and field staff had proposed to have one common poster that would identify the campaign

COMERCIO CON JUSTICIA:
MIS DERECHOS
NO SE NEGOCIAN

La globalización introdujo a millones de
mujeres pobres en la cadena productiva,
pero vulnera sus derechos fundamentales.
Apoye la campaña mundial Comercio con
Justicia por los derechos de las trabajadoras

COMERCIO
CON
JUSTICIA
www.comercioconjusticia.com

OXFAM INTERNACIONAL • CACTUS • RED GENERO Y COMERCIO • SISMA MUJER • C.U.T • NUEVA REPÚBLICA
TRIBUNAL NACIONAL MUJERES Y DESC • E.N.S. • C.C.J. • ILSA • ISMAC • C.G.T.D. • G.A.P. • MESA MUJERES Y ECONOMÍA • C.T.C

This is the Colombia campaign poster. The slogan reads: 'Make trade fair –
my rights are not negotiable'.
Source: MTF – My Rights are Not Negotiable

across the world. The Creative Services Unit at Oxfam GB developed a proposal that showed the hands of a worker, damaged by pesticides, with a backdrop of a dusty rural road. When this image was circulated for consultation, field staff roundly criticised the poster, particularly the fact that it only showed the woman's hands, rather than her face, and her problem – being a victim of pesticides – rather than her actions. The poster that was eventually developed includes the Oxfam green border on the top and the bottom (where alliance members' names or logos could be interchanged, maintaining the Make Trade Fair logo on one side). In the middle there are six different photographs, all of different women involved in different types of work. All photographs include the faces of the women, and they are from all over the world, of different ages, origins, and ethnicities, and working in very different industries. There is an overlay of a woman's symbol on several versions. It was agreed that each country could change one photograph and include an image that was clearly from their own country. These women are portrayed as protagonists.

Every single step, from the identification of the problem to the implementation of the campaign, must be taken considering the specificity of women as distinct from men. Analysing the impact of a problem, promoting a slogan or image, and developing a proposal must all be informed by the often invisible relationships between men and women that are mediated by their respective positions and power in society. Who does what? Who has what? Who decides? How and at what moments? Who wins and who loses? In addition to explicit analysis, strategies, and proposals, the way any alliance works will affect the general awareness about gender equality in the organisations that are members of the alliance. If men and women are equal, valued, and empowered in the member organisations, everyone will see gender equality in practice as well as hearing about it in theory. This can have a profound effect on the member organisations, the constituency of the alliance, the general public, and decision-makers.

Workers

In Nicaragua, over 68,000 people worked in *maquilas* in 2005. Eight-five per cent of this labour force is made up of women between the ages of 20 and 35; 45 per cent of them are single mothers and/or heads of household with an average of two or three children. The majority of the jobs is in the textile and garment industry, which is also a major employer of women workers in Morocco and Sri Lanka. In Morocco there are more than 220,000 workers in the textile and garment sector, and 71 per cent of them are women. In Sri Lanka, there are 273,603 workers in the garment industry, of which 80 per cent are women. Here, as elsewhere, some women workers in the garment industry are the primary earners in their family, so it is important that they earn a living wage – that they are not paid on the assumption that their wage supplements the income brought in by a male head of household.

In Colombia, women are employed in industries such as cut flowers, agriculture for export, services, and textiles. The cut-flower industry is now the number one non-traditional export industry. It is a labour-intensive industry, and employs about 80,000 people, of which the majority is female labour. As well as the common problems of low pay, insecurity of employment, poor health and safety, and so on (women earn 14 per cent less than men, and fewer than 35 per cent of women have access to social security), women workers face a cultural problem. Many people have the deeply rooted notion that women's earnings are secondary, that women work because they want to, and that what they earn is always supplementary to the earnings of a man. This belief is not confined to Colombia.

An individual example from Sri Lanka gives a sense of the difficulties women workers face due to the insecurity of their employment. The woman's identity is made anonymous to protect her privacy. Mrs SK is 43 years old and the sole breadwinner for their family of four because her husband is ill. She was a machine operator at a garment factory, which closed down without any notice in June 2005 due to lack of orders. None of the workers in the factory were paid any compensation, and their outstanding wages were unpaid. When interviewed in December 2005, Mrs SK had been unable to find another job because of her age, reflecting the bias of the industry towards young, unmarried workers.

Women workers experience disadvantage, discrimination, and oppression in many aspects of their lives – at home, in the community, in the political system, as well as at work. Alliances reaching out to women workers may recognise this and discuss rights in a wider context than the workplace.

The labour force in North Carolina that FLOC worked with was 98 per cent male. As migrant workers, their vulnerability was similar to that experienced by women workers: that is, precarious, temporary employment, lack of protection from labour laws, and inequality in power relations. The women in the labour camps did some of the same jobs as the men. Often, they would also perform non-field work like cooking, cleaning, and maintenance of the camp. In the fields, the women worked on crops that organisers and farm workers said were 'lighter', like tomatoes and chillies, and they would also drive machinery.

The male workers came from a 'macho' culture in Mexico.

FLOC had to deal with issues of sexual harassment of women by some male workers. Union organisers carried out mediation and education related to gender-equality issues and women's rights in the USA and Mexico.

Macho ideas about rugged individuals, able to do things on their own without help, were a potential impediment to organising the workers. The solution was to emphasise another aspect of the male role: to protect and feed their families. FLOC presented mistreatment by growers and exploitation by Mt. Olive as obstacles to the male workers' desire to provide for their family. This approach provided a safe environment in which the men could accept the support and leadership of FLOC. The union presented its case to Mt. Olive, NCGA, the media, churches, and other allies in the same way: health, safety, money, working conditions, and other concerns were framed as 'family issues'.

FLOC staff had anecdotal evidence that increased wages led to increases in the amount of money sent home. Women in Mexico have told FLOC organisers that they are grateful for the increases and other benefits to the workers and their families. In the words of one organiser:

'So we can assume workers are sending the money back to Mexico. Workers are always railing and complaining about how they can't send money back. They rarely complain that they're hungry and always refer to their families in informal conversations. Some will keep it but as a whole most of them send the money home'.

FLOC organisers also felt that their work helped to change the male workers' perceptions of relationships between women and men. Because local FLOC leaders were women there was much more respect for the capacity and work of women in the fields, in the community and in general. To illustrate this change, one organiser shared the story of how, after the Mt. Olive and NCGA victory, one worker asked NCGA leaders in an informal meeting: 'Why aren't women in the programme? Why don't women come in and work for NCGA?'

Finally, FLOC also had to deal with issues of specific concern to female farm workers, such as access to bathrooms, and privacy issues arising from the husband–wife relationship. For example, FLOC reported having to intervene in cases where married couples had to sleep in the same room with other men. After holding discussions with the workers, the couples got moved to different, more private housing.

Women's-rights organisations

As we saw when discussing alliances, women's organisations formed the nucleus of the alliance in Morocco, and a women's organisation led the alliance in Nicaragua. In Sri Lanka, the majority of the organisations making up the alliance had been engaged with women workers before joining the alliance. In Colombia and Morocco, however, the women's movement had focused more on civil rights than on labour rights (with a few notable exceptions) before the alliance was formed. Whatever issues the organisations tackled – legal rights, domestic violence, sexual health, or family planning – there is a common thread of empowering women, which is also key to campaigning on labour rights. The organisations saw women's rights at work in the context of women's rights at home and in the wider society. Their perspective is that it is essential to change public perception of the value of women and women's work (both in the household and in their work sites), in society and amongst decision-makers, in order to have effective regulation.

The staff, volunteers, and activists of women's organisations were also likely to be empowered and highly aware of gender-equality issues themselves, as compared with people in the wider society and even in the NGO sector. The growth of personal awareness and confidence through participation in the campaign can be seen as a welcome side effect. The alliance in Colombia agreed to rotate leadership roles so that women who were beginning to develop leadership skills would gain experience as spokeswomen for the campaign. Each woman had a main role in an activity while the others formed a support team; then one of the support team would take a turn as spokeswoman, and so on. Leadership passed on like a baton in a relay race. Two women from Colombia report:

> *I slowly started to discover myself as a woman in that group, and to understand the life of women. I grew as a human being and as a leader.*
>
> *The campaign became a militant opportunity for each of us, we wove networks of affection. Tuesday meetings became a space for celebration and joy. I grew a great deal as a leader and as a woman. I feel it and people tell me so.*

Gender equality in the alliances

Other members of the alliances – typically trade unions in many cases – were often much less aware of gender-equality issues. Often male-dominated organisations, with a constituency of a largely male unionised workforce, they tended to see little distinction between women's labour rights and labour rights in general. The influence of these organisations in the alliance's decision-making can have the effect of pushing women's issues and the gender perspective down the agenda, or off it altogether.

When the alliance in Morocco was planning to meet the employment minister, members had a discussion about how to prioritise messaging in a limited amount of time with the campaign's key target. Members made a tactical decision not to focus exclusively on 'women's issues' (maternity leave, breaks for breast-feeding, nurseries for children, sexual harassment) during this first encounter, because the broader message they wanted to convey to the government was that it was important to put in place specific measures to promote enforcement of the new labour code.

The alliance chose to highlight five 'new' provisions in the code that, if adequately enforced, had the potential to strengthen women's rights: a higher minimum wage, shorter weekly working hours, the introduction of health and safety committees in factories, the creation of a medical service for workers, and the conditions to regulate temporary contracts. The first two issues (a higher minimum wage and respecting legal working hours) clearly benefit women in their socially assigned caring roles, but are also important for men. But for women, working hours are key. Many women workers complain that when their boss asks them unexpectedly to stay extra hours and doesn't allow them to call home, this creates problems with their husbands (who get suspicious or worry about safety on the way back home at night). It also means that another woman in the family (sister or daughter) has to take over evening domestic chores.

The middle two issues (the introduction of health and safety committees in factories and the creation of a medical service for workers) are more broadly applicable to all workers, and the last issue (regulating temporary contracts) provides greater protection to women workers simply because they are the majority in temporary contractual arrangements. In fact, the five points are strategically more important for women workers because they focus on women's socially assigned roles (and challenge the employers and government to assume the costs of women workers being in the workplace) whereas the 'female specific issues' are limited to women's reproductive roles. While those last points are important, they are more tactical. Women cannot 'skip' maternity leave or not breast-feed, for example.

In one country, the alliance decided to invite a well-known women's organisation to join them. This, they thought, would enhance the campaign's gender dimension, mainly because the women's organisation could help develop policy positions based on a sound analysis from a gender perspective. Also, the alliance wanted to encourage the women's movement to get more involved in advocating labour rights where their focus has traditionally been on civil rights. Members believed that the entry of this new organisation could reinforce the alliance's profile and capacities significantly and balance out internal differences, acting as a catalyst. The organisation has not joined the alliance yet, however.

In another country, a women's organisation in the alliance found that reproductive health was not prioritised as a main campaign objective. 'From our very inception we were talking about reproductive health. But it did not emerge as an issue in these discussions.' Other alliance members considered that it could be included within a broader problem statement and the women's organisations acquiesced. In retrospect, they admit that they didn't negotiate the issue well: 'That was a mistake committed on our part'. Reproductive health is not an issue that a labour-rights campaign needs to address. However, organisations that had been conducting certain training programmes and were attractive to workers felt that their agenda items needed to be included in the campaign plan. This shows the difficulty in reconciling different interests of diverse organisations, which sometimes include their priorities in a broader campaign simply for survival.

In Colombia, right at the beginning of the efforts to build the alliance, an organisation of rural women workers wanted to participate actively in the alliance, but agreed to do so only if their particular situation was expressly included in all the public materials. Women in rural areas are sometimes small producers, artisans, waged workers on large plantations, or do work as payment 'in kind' for their neighbours. Their situation is very varied and informal. The other alliance members became concerned because they felt that the campaign could only gain legitimacy if the alliance was able to back up their arguments with statistical information and rigorous studies. That kind of information was not available on the situation of rural women workers. This caused tension, until the rural women's organisations recognised that the kind of information necessary was not available and the other alliance members created a 'second channel' of participation, where the rural women workers' organisation was invited to broader events, but does not form part of the co-ordination team.

The alliance in Sri Lanka had difficulty in obtaining the representation of women members from trade unions in spite of the alliance insisting on this requirement. This is primarily because these trade unions don't have many female staff.

By contrast, the alliance in Nicaragua, led by a women's organisation, was able to agree on a training programme for women workers that mixed gender equality, sexual and reproductive health, and family planning with labour rights and health and safety in the workplace. This must be seen as the result of 12 years work on gender-equality issues – 12 years ago, such a programme would not have been easy to agree on. The centrality of gender equality in the campaign is summed up in the regional campaign slogan 'employment yes – but with dignity'. In the alliance's analysis, the assaults on the dignity of women workers in *maquilas* include verbal violence, non-compliance with labour laws and regulations, sexual harassment and sexual abuse, among other problems.

The balance in Colombia is more delicate. The initial core group was made up of women's organisations, but in the words of one of the co-ordinators:

'No sooner had we got together than we realised that a campaign for labour rights would not make any sense without the participation of the trade unions'.

They approached the women's secretariats of the trade unions with great caution, being careful not to hurt the sensitivities of male trade-union leaders who were not very happy about being in the back row. Within the Colombian trade unions, men have usually been in charge, and women have been subordinate. It was not easy for the male leaders to agree to participate in a campaign in which the trade-union cause was not the main one, and in which women in the trade union would be the contacts with the rest of the alliance. However, after many meetings and much persuasion the two largest national trade unions, *Central Unitaria de Trabajadores* (Unified Workers Union) and *Central General de Trabajadores* (General Workers Union), agreed to send women representatives to join the alliance.

The relationship was soon tested. The alliance planned to use 8 March, International Women's Day, for a demonstration about women workers' rights. They included the main trade unions in the plans. A day before the event, the male trade-union leaders called to say that everything was ready but that they wanted to know at what moment they would be able to go on stage as they wanted to greet the women on their day. The organisers told them 'no thanks, the stage is reserved for the women, it is our day. We are not celebrating May Day'. The march took place, and when the crowd arrived at the Bolivar Square the male trade-union leaders again asked to come up on the stage. But then, each and every woman replied with a categorical 'this is our day' and said that if the trade unions wanted to speak up they could do so through the women trade-union representatives who were part of the campaign. Reluctantly, the male leaders accepted. And for the first time, at a rally where the trade unions were present, the only voices were those of the women. After this day, the relationship with the women trade-union leaders was not as smooth, but a precedent was set which will be helpful in future joint actions.

The balance between 'worker' and 'women' perspectives is not fixed. Discussions within the alliances give women's organisations the opportunity to show other members the importance of a gender perspective.

In this, they may find allies in the women's departments of trade unions, finding common cause with women who sometimes feel marginalised in their own organisation. At best, a dialogue can take place: women's organisations can learn how to add labour rights to the other rights that women should have; and trade unions can learn about the distinctive and additional problems of women workers.

Women from mixed organisations faced challenges when participating in alliances. In addition to doing the external lobbying work that was part of the strategy, many had to carry out internal lobbying work towards their own organisations so that they would give the campaign, and the issues, the necessary attention, resources, and backing. This is also true in many international organisations, including Oxfam. Their participation in the alliances has resulted in their own empowerment, but it has also brought greater profile to the respective organisations as they have moved into new arenas. This empowerment isn't without its tensions, because the campaigns then become a catalyst for gauging how real the institutional commitments of NGOs, trade unions, universities, and alliance members to gender equality really are; and to what extent those commitments translate into practical expressions such as time, resources, people, or backing.

Institutional arrangements can be made to alter the balance within an alliance. From the start of the alliance in Sri Lanka, each member was asked to nominate two representatives to the alliance membership, one being a woman. This was done with a view to encouraging female representation and participation from trade unions and encouraging more female activists in the sector. Despite this, female members of ALaRM say that the voice of women was restrained in the initial months of discussions. The alliance subsequently addressed this issue by giving support and priority to female members to express their opinions and views. The tactics varied according to circumstances. At times, women were specifically invited to express their views in the context of mixed conversations in meetings; at other times, in informal group conversations outside the meetings (for example, while walking). The leaders encouraged women to talk about a particular issue and then gently encouraged them to express the same opinions within the meeting place, emphasising that practice would bring confidence. Occasionally, women were encouraged to discuss their viewpoints at home, with their partners.

FLOC has, since passing a resolution on gender equality in 1986, tried to practise equality between men and women in hiring, benefits, and other issues. Most of FLOC's organising directors are women, about half of all organisers are women, and most camp representatives are women. It should also be mentioned that a majority of the church supporters of the campaign were older, often retired, women.

Gender equality played an important role in the distribution of responsibilities and building of trust between workers and FLOC organisers. Visits to the labour camps, where the overwhelming majority of the residents were men, yielded interesting images of workers warmly greeting FLOC organisers as respected younger union sisters who had much information and humanity to support the workers. Women organisers, like FLOC's organising director Leticia Zavala and community member Angelita Morrisroe, earned the trust and respect of the male workers by listening to their workplace issues such as non-payment of wages, bad working conditions, and problems with work visas, and providing solutions to these problems. Some solutions that they provided were: help in collecting unpaid wages, getting drinking water into the fields, and arranging access to legal council to resolve visa issues. Once this leadership status was established through producing concrete gains, the fact that the organisers were women became irrelevant.

In Morocco, the fact that five out of six members are represented by women has strengthened the campaign's focus on labour rights in sectors that employ mostly women, such as the clothing sector. Members found that an alliance consisting of women representatives can be more sensitive to women's issues and to women workers' particular needs. Including women unionists in the group has been positive because it has helped strengthen their position, and their interest in women's rights, in male-dominated unions.

Summary

Gender equality is central to any work on development issues. The key is to ask ourselves if our work is helping us to move purposefully (not accidentally) towards greater gender equality. Women have rights. If any of their rights are violated, then the individuals and the wider community are the poorer. Development benefits from the recognition and exercise of women's rights – indeed, the recognition and exercise of women's rights is often the most important development that can take place. Every time a woman becomes aware of this and speaks out, that is a gain for herself and for the wider community.

Organisations which join or form alliances to campaign on women's labour rights are likely to have a background and perspective which emphasises either 'labour' or 'women'. No matter what the issue, each side should be prepared to learn from the other, to help create a campaign which reaches out to its constituency both as women and as workers. There will also be long-term benefits in making women workers, trade unions, NGOs, and other members of civil society more aware of gender-equality issues. Even where the alliance works with an overwhelmingly male constituency, as in the case study from the USA, there are opportunities to work in a way that respects gender equality and helps men become more aware of gender-equality issues. From the gender perspective, it is important to gather data which is broken down according to gender and to gather individual case studies; and to look at the different experiences of women and men, whatever the focus of your campaign.

Key points

- Incorporate gender-equality considerations not just in the aims of the work but in the way it is carried out. This ensures that the campaign will have a positive impact on the power relations between women and men.

- When preparing the campaign strategy, be sure to include not only policy goals but parallel goals that can be just as important, such as highlighting women as agents of change (instead of victims), portraying men and women in roles that challenge common myths, and involving women in ways that allow them to develop new and non-traditional skills.

- Never presume that all organisations share the same experience and depth of gender analysis. Discussions within alliances give women's organisations the opportunity to share their gender analysis with others, including women who may feel marginalised within their own organisations.

- Work to ensure that the specificity of men and women is valued, and women's invisibility is overcome.

- Remember that incorporating a gender perspective can be a process that produces tension, since it becomes a catalyst for gauging the real weight of an institution's commitment to gender equality and how it translates into practice.

- Facilitate continuous dialogue on gender between member organisations of the alliance; this will promote gender equality within the campaign, and the improved awareness will have long-term benefits for other campaigns.

5 • Using the media

Overview

The benefits of good media work include:

- raising public awareness of the issue, to prepare the ground for mobilisation;
- bringing the debate into the open, to back up lobbying;
- putting pressure on stakeholders;
- and informing and reassuring women workers, members of the alliance, and the wider NGO community that the campaign is happening and scoring successes.

Effective media work involves:

- having a media strategy;
- agreeing a set of clear messages that run throughout the campaign that can be adapted to different situations;
- arranging press releases, press conferences, and photo opportunities;
- cultivating journalists;
- creating opportunities for media coverage;
- reacting to opportunities that arise;
- and targeting particular stories to relevant audiences through specific media.

The media

A country's mass media consist of newspapers ('the press'), the broadcast media (radio and television), and, increasingly, electronic media such as websites, electronic newsletters, and online discussion groups. They can be further divided into national and regional; and serious or popular. In some countries the media may operate in more than one language. These considerations affect what kind of story a particular paper or station will pick up, and what audience it will reach.

Conventional media work consists of providing journalists with your story, hoping that they run it, and trusting that they tell it accurately. Greater control of the message can be achieved by using paid advertising, and by creating and distributing your own materials. There are additional channels for reaching the public, through popular entertainment – films and music, and their stars – and literature.

The media often share, and express, social prejudices and preconceptions – for instance, the gender stereotypes discussed earlier. All alliances face varying degrees of elite control of the media, which makes access difficult. But some areas of the media will be more penetrable than others, and a media strategy should identify and focus on them. The alliance in Colombia held a workshop to analyse the media and the power behind it, and where it might be possible to penetrate the elite control. MEC in Nicaragua and FLOC in the USA had a long history of media work and had developed the necessary analysis and contacts.

Press releases

The media work of the Moroccan alliance is a good example of a strategy that relies heavily on press releases. They sent out seven releases between March 2005 and March 2006. These were issued on certain key dates, for example May Day and International Women's Day, or when there was a particular event, for example in response to a government announcement or a national conference on employment policy. For instance, after the meeting with the employment minister discussed above, the alliance sent out a press release summarising the key points discussed during the meeting. This press release aimed to engage the government publicly in the points they had agreed.

Key messages for planned press releases were usually agreed through group discussions at strategic planning meetings (every three months). One member drafted the press release, and the others reviewed and approved it in accordance with set deadlines. Releases were sent to newspapers which: had the greatest readership; had an editorial stance close to the alliance's position; were ones where the alliance members had a contact.

Press releases have not always received the expected coverage. In one case the press published an article on the basis of an alliance press release but using a completely different style from the original text, which twisted its content and message. In another case, the press release failed to get the expected coverage because it was not well-prepared: the text was too long, it was sent to the press too late to be included in the planned issue, and it was not followed up systematically with the newspaper/journalists who were supposed to print it.

Following this unsuccessful attempt, the alliance set out to prepare better press releases. One of the most successful cases was a press release that received unprecedented coverage and attracted a lot of attention for a combination of reasons: it was a good, concise document; it was about a 'hot' issue (there was a disagreement between the government, employers, and unions on how to raise the minimum wage and the alliance added its voice to the debate); it was a swift response to an announcement made by the prime minister (in fact the only civil-society response to the announcement); its timing was good, as the press release was sent during a particularly quiet period, in July 2005; and it was properly followed up with the journalists to ensure that it was published.

The alliance in Colombia faced an additional difficulty in getting the media to take notice of press releases: because of the continuing violence in the country, journalists do not give much coverage to information about anything else. The alliance concluded that it must write documents that were easy reading material for journalists with a hectic work pace, and that they must meet four other requirements: to show evidence of the situation, to have full names and faces, to include statistics, and to put forward concrete proposals. If they did not meet these requirements, they would not offer it to be published. A bonus effect of this approach was the encouragement it gave to those workers whose case studies were published. A worker in the cut-flower industry reported:

> *We were thrilled about the fact that our situation was being portrayed in the newspapers, on television, on the radio. It gave us support to continue fighting for our rights not to be violated, to recover what we have lost.*

Press conferences

A step up from press releases, in terms of the preparation needed and the potential for getting good coverage, is a press conference or press briefing. Good preparation gets good results. Before their very first press conference, the appointed spokespeople of one alliance held practice sessions. They also arranged the seating to put friendly supporters closer, and prompted specific people to be in the audience to ask key questions that would help get their messages across. An example of an effective press conference comes from Sri Lanka. ALaRM organised a press briefing in December 2005 to share the 'Draft MFA impact analysis,' a report outlining the impact of the MFA phase-out on the Sri Lankan apparel industry. The alliance backed up the research by inviting women workers who had lost their jobs to give personal testimonies. This combination attracted a lot of attention and coverage from the media. When the labour minister read newspaper reports of factory closures and the impact on workers, he instructed the department to confirm the truth of these reports.

In Colombia the alliance combined public actions like demonstrations with press conferences. They invited key political leaders to the demonstrations, and told journalists that the leaders would be there. This has been a useful way to do press conferences, but the problem is that most of the time the media covers the leaders' speeches and not the popular action.

The location of a press conference can be symbolic of the campaign itself. FLOC press conferences seized the imagination of journalists by being organised around the pool table in *La Palmita*, the grocery-store headquarters of its campaign. This served to back up the message that the campaign was rooted in, and supported by, the local community. On the other hand, MEC held a press conference in a large convention centre, with the participation of an Oxfam representative, the head of the free trade zone, the labour minister and the president of INSS. Many women workers also attended. This showed that the campaign was a serious effort, with support from various sectors.

Events

As we have seen, some alliances organised public events such as the International Women's Day celebration in Colombia and May Day in Sri Lanka. These can be seen as mobilisations of the workers, but of course they are also newsworthy events in themselves, and speeches by representatives of the alliance give an opportunity to get the message across to journalists covering the story. As well as the 'foreground' story, that the event took place, and what the speakers said, there are also several 'background' messages for journalists: that the alliance is professional and effective enough to organise a major public event; that the alliance is a likely source of further interesting stories; and that women can march and speak in public as confidently as men.

In Sri Lanka the alliance celebrated May Day with a procession which included a mixture of cultural pageantry items that made it more appealing to the workers. This idea was taken up by the women's organisations which were celebrating International Women's Day. About 30 women's organisations (including some ALaRM members) had a procession in the free trade zone on the evening of 8 March, focusing the attention of the authorities on the issue of insecurity for women workers in the zone. Though not an ALaRM event itself, it is an example of creativity that generated a lot of media coverage.

Members of free trade zones and General Services Employees Union (a member organisation of ALaRM) holding their organisation banner at the ALaRM May Day in Sri Lanka, 2005. Source: ALaRM Campaign, Katunayake, 2005

Other events may bring alliance organisers into contact with journalists. Alliance members in Morocco who were attending a conference, running a stall, and distributing their brochure, were able to create a media opportunity because a journalist from an Arab cable-television station became interested in the campaign and interviewed them.

Publicity stunts can be an option for campaigners. During the May Day celebrations in Honduras, a member of an Oxfam-supported alliance put out a moving float with live models to illustrate the speed with which the workers had to produce their shirts.

Visual images

All the media except, of course, radio, need visual images. The guarantee, or even the promise, of an interesting picture is likely to attract journalists to a press conference, and it is one of the attractions of an event. Campaigning often consists of people sitting in meetings, and the excitement of what they are saying or hearing does not translate into an exciting picture. A photograph of a worker, with a caption giving her name and story (or the worker speaking directly to the television camera), is a much more attractive package for journalists. All the alliances took digital photographs of events, to make available to journalists even in press releases. Here, as with press releases in general, quality is more important than quantity: the ideal is a well-composed, high-resolution photograph of a person who is named and quoted, and whose personal story ties into the campaign theme.

Cultivating links with journalists

Over several years, MEC in Nicaragua established a fruitful relationship with journalists, based on a mutual interest in promoting women *maquila* workers' rights. This relationship has been built over time through previous media campaigns. It has succeeded due to a common identification between the aims of MEC in favour of women workers' rights and the personal vision of the journalists – and because the journalists respect MEC as an organisation that works through educational and campaigning activities rather than confrontation.

MEC promoted a training process specifically aimed at 29 men and women journalists from different communications media. They discussed topics such as: the bill for establishing the general law of labour hygiene and safety in Nicaragua and the social-security law; sexually transmitted infectious diseases; the aims and reach of the campaign; and self-esteem, among others. The idea was to ensure that journalists had first-hand information about the campaign and its activities, in order to broadcast news in a more informed way. All the participants valued this as a very positive experience. This strengthened MEC's relationship with national journalists, and it contributed greatly to creating a favourable attitude in the media towards the campaign.

Oxfam supported the Moroccan alliance by browsing the press for media coverage and interesting events or other issues of relevance, and by identifying key journalists and occasions for potential press releases. As part of the alliance's growing self-reliance, members are now proposing to organise a meeting with journalists to introduce and explain the campaign – 'so that they know what we do'. Members propose that the alliance should prepare a press pack to distribute, or organise a round-table meeting. There have been a couple of small or bilateral meetings with journalists, but no official meeting which could also establish a network of contacts. In order to start a proper media strategy, members also suggest creating a small team of two or three people within the alliance who will act as focal points, establish the network of media contacts, and co-ordinate all media work.

In Sri Lanka, journalists self-selected. The alliance issued wide invitations to briefings and events. Subsequently, those who were interested in the issue closely followed up, and the alliance provided them with additional information as and when required.

FLOC staff in the USA developed close relationships with local media professionals in print and electronic media. This created more fertile ground on which regular press releases, press conferences, and other media events would be received. The content of the media events included 'know your rights' information, denunciations of specific practices in labour camps, reports of deaths and injuries among workers, and other issues. A major problem identified by FLOC staff was the frequency with which reporters were transferred, moved, or removed from their area whenever they actually began to understand and report more extensively on the issue. FLOC staff stated that, in some cases, media professionals believed they would be punished or negatively impacted by 'getting too close' to the Mt. Olive campaign. So FLOC began to systematically cultivate two or three people working for each newspaper or radio station they were trying to reach. Building and maintaining relationships with numerous media professionals in the same newspaper, radio, or television station created conditions that would keep FLOC and workers' issues high on the agenda of the editorial and news rooms of the various local and national media outlets.

Having close relationships with journalists can also help an alliance learn more proactively about the effectiveness – or not – of your media work. Call journalists to ask about their coverage, what else they might need, and ways to improve.

Do it yourself

There are many other ways of getting a message across to your target audience, in addition to conventional media work. Many of them have the advantage that the alliance has more control over the content and timing. A distinction can be made between two types of media coverage. 'Earned' coverage is gained from press releases, press conferences, and events, and backed up by cultivating journalists. 'Placed' coverage includes editorials, opinion pieces, and paid advertisements. The different approaches require different types of contacts with the press, different inputs, and have different costs. The examples in this section are based on work done by national alliances that had considerable financial support. A third category includes different ways of by-passing the mass media altogether.

FLOC communicated with the workers in the labour camps by writing, printing, and distributing *Boletin* – a mini-newspaper of about six pages. They distributed this monthly between May and October in laundromats, grocery stores, and other local sites near labour camps. FLOC workers in Mexico also distributed *Boletin* during the farm-worker recruitment period between January and May. The union also used email to provide regular updates to individual and organisational supporters. The updates included reports, picket activities, victories, working conditions, the state of the campaign, and so on.

The campaign in Nicaragua made great use of paid advertisements. This was the first time that a social organisation had done so in such an extended way. Specifically, they had: 189 spots on seven television channels with national coverage and three cable channels with municipal coverage; 7,788 30-second radio clips during 47 radio programmes on 27 stations; 3,969 film spots in seven cinemas in Managua, selected for being the most visited; and articles published in paid spaces in two magazines, which ensured that they would be seen by certain audiences, particularly those in government and the business sector.

Advertising gave the alliance control of the content, and they did much to share this control with women workers. The contents of each of the messages were discussed and approved by women workers, who were consulted about them through the use of focus groups. Workers who are involved in MEC's ongoing programmes were consulted. They are workers from the free trade zone, and most were under the age of 30. Their level of engagement varied, but they all participated in training, and in annual national events called colloquiums. The content of the cable-television spots in Estelí and Juigalpa involved the particular conditions of women workers in both places; in Estelí they focused on working conditions for women in the tobacco industry, whereas in Juigalpa they focused on women in non-industrialised mining. The spots screened on national television and in cinemas featured *maquila* workers as actors, instead of professional actors, and the ones in the textile sector were filmed inside an actual factory. All of the messages promoted equality for women by demanding respect for labour and health rights as well as better physical conditions in the workplace.

Several alliances printed materials of their own, although the scale and use varied widely. We have seen that the alliance in Sri Lanka printed a leaflet to explain and support the signature-petition mobilisation. They knew that many leaflets and newspapers are distributed to the free trade zone workers and they are usually thrown away unread. ALaRM distributed their leaflet along with a colourful telephone index with details of laws and regulations governing garment-industry workers, to capture the attention of the workers so they would keep them. In Nicaragua, the alliance printed 30,000 pocket-book manuals on safety procedures in the workplace. They also made posters, signs, and banners with the messages of the campaign. The manuals were given to women and men workers in the *maquilas* and the posters were placed in the special zone factories, in public buildings, and in collective spaces such as bus stops.

The alliance in Colombia developed a video for the campaign launch showing women workers, and later a five-minute DVD of cinema quality outlining the issues. It has been presented in massive public events, both alliance events and joint events such as the Day of Action Against Poverty (as part of the Global Call to Action Against Poverty). It is a quick, attractive way to get the message across and give visibility to their slogan, logo, and alliance.

The alliance in Morocco produced a brochure setting out the campaign's analysis and advocacy agenda. This was distributed to key political targets in the ministries of labour and industry, as well as to Morocco's two employers' federations. Unions distributed the brochure internally and other members of the alliance distributed it among their constituents. Oxfam published two case studies on Spanish clothing companies' purchasing practices in Morocco and their impact on women workers' conditions (*Moda que Aprieta* – 'The High Price of Fashion' – and *Marcando Tendencias* — 'Setting the Trend'). These studies were based on the findings that emerged during several focus groups with workers from Tangiers' free trade zone. Alliance members participated in the focus groups, which was an opportunity to learn about how buyers' purchasing practices affect labour conditions in suppliers' factories.

This poster about health and safety appeals to the business sense of Nicaragua's factory owners and the good sense of the workers. It argues that prevention is cheap, and productivity can be maintained if health and safety criteria are addressed. It was used throughout the campaign in conjunction with cinema and radio advertisements. Source: MEC and RSTN, 2004

This 2005 brochure was produced as part of the Morocco campaign for public education and awareness-raising. The brochure analyses the situation of women workers, explains the application of the 2005 labour code, and includes recommendations from the alliance. It has been successfully used throughout the campaign with civil-society organisations. Source: Intermón Oxfam and ADT, March 2005

Using the media

It is always useful for publicity purposes if the campaign can have a distinctive identity. FLOC referred to the 'Mt. Olive Campaign' instead of the 'North Carolina Growers' Association Campaign' because it is the brand name of the major buyer, which makes it susceptible to consumer pressure. The alliance in Sri Lanka had a name – ALaRM – and a logo. The campaign in Morocco was called *Campagne nationale pour l'application effective de la legislation du travail* (National campaign for labour-law enforcement) and it was carried out by the *Alliance pour les Droits des Travailleuses* (Alliance for Women Workers' Rights). The alliance is also proposing to adopt a logo. Nicaragua and Colombia both have slogans: *El Trabajo y la Salud Laboral es…¡Mi Derecho!* ('Workplace health and safety is…my right!') and *Mis Derechos No Se Negocian* ('My rights are not negotiable') respectively.

Individuals can have great significance in raising the profile of a campaign. We have already seen how the Colombia campaign engaged in debate with a prominent media commentator, and also made use of celebrity supporters. Best of all is for individuals from alliance member organisations to put the argument directly. Marta Cecilia Londoño, from the *Escuela Nacional Sindical de Medellín*, appeared on a regional television programme and was able to challenge the idea that women's earnings are secondary. In Nicaragua, people from MEC and other members of the alliance appeared on four television programmes, discussing the campaign.

Appropriate media

Effective media work uses different media for different audiences at different moments for different reasons. To put the options very simply: ordinary people get their news from the broadcast media, and you can help to get your story into the broadcast media by using human-interest stories and celebrities; decision-makers read serious newspapers, and you can help to get your story into these newspapers by providing well-thought-out policy positions backed by research and statistics. To give just one example of the choice in action, we can look at Morocco. In a country like Morocco, where illiteracy rates are high, radio and television can have a much greater impact than the press, which only reaches the educated elite. So far, however, the allies have concentrated on the press, because the campaign's main target was the government, and they read the written press.

In Nicaragua, the USA, and Colombia, the websites of partners and allies housed information about the campaigns; in Sri Lanka, the organisations found websites costly to establish and maintain so they did not use this medium, instead prioritising other channels. In many countries there is very limited access to the Internet, making it an inappropriate campaigning tool. However, the technology is changing fast, access is increasing, and costs are coming down, so it is worth considering the Internet as a campaigning tool.

Summary

There is a wide range of ways to use the media. At the simplest, the alliance sends out press releases; more ambitious strategies include organising press conferences, cultivating journalists, and a range of actions described under the heading 'Do it yourself'. The options available depend on the country's media. The decision about which option to use should rest on how media work can contribute to the overall campaign strategy. It will also depend on the state of the media in the country, the resources at the disposal of the organisations, and their access to original research that will maximise media impact.

Key points

- Carry out a power analysis of all media, including electronic channels, as well as the best ways to penetrate them (such as through celebrities, or stunts that act as attention-getting techniques).

- Remember that individuals can have great significance in raising the profile of a campaign. Personal testimonies, articulate alliance members, and well-known national personalities can all be attractive in various types of media.

- Be aware that effective media work engages the people who have the power to help the campaign achieve its intended goal. Though it may be easier to penetrate popular media, it may be more beneficial to get a campaign message in a medium that reaches the necessary decision-makers.

- Ask yourselves the following questions: whom do you want to reach, with what messages, what do you want them to do, which part of the media is the best way to reach them, and when? Your campaign strategy should help you to be clear about what you want to say to which of your target audiences, and why.

- Remember that media work should not be an end in itself. It should only be undertaken if it contributes effectively to the overall campaign strategy.

6 • Developing policy

Overview

Campaigning organisations increasingly find that they need to go beyond identifying and publicising problems, to develop legitimate, alternative policy solutions. If your alliance merely complains, the target institutions – government, employers, the serious media – can justifiably respond by asking what you, the complainers, would do instead. If you leave policy formation to the target institutions, you will always be on the back foot, responding and reacting, when you could be leading the debate and setting the agenda. We have seen that lobbying can often be a co-operative exercise between NGOs and the government, or at least need not be confrontational, and ministers and civil servants will look favourably on an alliance which shows it is serious and propositional, and offers concrete policy proposals.

Research

Research is often the beginning of the process of policy formulation – and even if it isn't, it is good to have some research to back up and add credibility to your position. Research can take several forms, from simply gathering data, case studies, and human-interest stories, to background analysis of the political context, policy trends, statistical information, and campaigns in other countries.

In Morocco, one of the members of the initial alliance (CDG) did a piece of research on the new labour code in 2004. Its results were presented to alliance members and other civil-society organisations at a conference which helped shape the campaign's initial recommendations. When the broader alliance was formed, the initial priority was to agree a common advocacy agenda. After the agenda was agreed, and published in the brochure, and the first meeting with the government had taken place, members realised that they needed more statistics and data to strengthen their lobbying:

> *When we tell the government that things are not working, that the law is not implemented, we need examples to show how many women workers were fired in this place, how many faced violations of their labour rights in that place, etc.*

As a result of this realisation, some members started collecting existing data from their organisation's archives, but this exercise proved problematic for several reasons. Data is sorted and classified differently by different organisations; it may be confidential; and it is not complete or comprehensive – it is only cases they happen to come across, or cases of women workers who contact the organisation and report their problem, but these may not be representative. Trade unions' data may not be representative, since only a small proportion of workers in the country are unionised. Finally, members do not necessarily have the time, resources, or expertise to dedicate to data collection and analysis. These difficulties led members to conclude that they needed to carry out research based on tailor-made questions that would respond to the campaign needs. The fundamental question that needs to be asked is: 'What kind of data does the campaign need?'

Oxfam also did its own research on the impact of Spanish companies' purchasing policies on women workers in Morocco's garment sector. It organised focus groups with women workers in 2003 and 2005 to collect data. This exercise was independent of the alliance's work, but alliance members were invited to participate in the focus-group discussions. A member of the alliance reported that this research helped them to see 'where the national campaign fits within a broader campaign that also targets multinational corporations'.

In Nicaragua, research with workers has been designed to feed into the policy-making process. Consultation carried out with women working in textiles, tobacco, and domestic work identified inadequacies in the country's labour code, and the causes of non-compliance. This information fed into the writing of the bill for a national occupational health and safety law, as described above. Women workers have also fed their views and experiences into the debate about the law for employment and dignified wages with a gender focus promoted by MEC. For example, in November 2005, more than 400 women living in the department of León participated in a debate-consultation on this proposal. By February 2006,

This is a programme for the annual colloquium, held on International Women's Day, 5 March 2006 in Managua, Nicaragua. Many Nicaraguan women gathered to have workshops, discuss the issues, and demand a gender perspective to be included in the national employment policy.
Source: MEC, 2006

the process of consultation had allowed more than 3,000 women (workers and others) to give their opinion and suggest recommendations on this policy initiative. MEC's final proposal was presented to the president of the republic during the Eighth Women's Colloquium, held in March 2006.

In Sri Lanka, the alliance conducted two pieces of research; one was a draft MFA impact analysis, particularly examining the impact on workers. The research showed that there were 15 factory closures during 2005, and that these had been carried out without following the standard legal procedures. With the exception of one factory, none paid any sort of legal compensation to the workers, and almost all the factories had enormous defaults for statutory payments. This was clearly a situation which should have been of concern to the Department of Labour. This was the first time that the actual number of closed factories, and the real impact of the MFA phase-out, came to light. Until that time, even the Department of Labour was unaware of the exact number of closures and the number of workers who had lost their jobs. The study prompted the minister to call for the department to carry out its own investigation. As we saw above, the alliance added an extra dimension to this research by including case studies of individual workers who had been affected by factory closures. The research from a worker perspective was well received by all stakeholders.

Of course, gathering case studies and human-interest stories from the labour force is also useful to provide information for supporters and the media, as we have seen from the campaigns in Colombia and the USA.

FLOC's campaign strategy rested on detailed knowledge of the supply chain, which identified Mt. Olive as a major buyer from NCGA. Mt. Olive enjoys brand recognition in the USA, which left them vulnerable to a consumer boycott. Once the campaign started, FLOC organisers met small groups of workers to brainstorm problems, solutions, and actions, writing everything down on flip-chart paper. These meetings have already been mentioned under the heading of 'training', because organisers used the opportunity to inform workers; they can also be seen as 'mobilisation', because they built up trust between organisers and workers, and made the rapid sign-up campaign possible. And because they identified small, achievable campaign objectives, they should also be seen as part of the policy process. As one of the organisers put it, the meetings enabled them to 'find something the workers were willing to fight for'.

Discussion

The alliance in Morocco found that developing joint policy recommendations was a challenging exercise, particularly for allies whose advocacy in the past had mainly focused on mobilisation. The campaign's initial advocacy agenda was developed through a collaborative process that resulted in the publication of a joint campaign brochure. The brochure's content was built up in two stages: a first stage of bilateral meetings during which each member met the campaign co-ordinator separately to set out their priority messages; and later a group meeting to discuss and agree on the broad thrust of the common draft. The result was a consensual document which all the members believed in and supported with enthusiasm.

Allies believe that the campaign's current proposals and recommendations are the most important ones they could propose at this stage, as they touch on fundamental issues. The campaign should stick to these proposals and they should be pursued until the alliance sees some tangible results. As a second phase, the campaign could build on this set of arguments and develop further policy points.

As part of Oxfam's leadership role in Morocco, they support the alliance's policy development by encouraging policy discussions, keeping records of agreements, identifying common points between the allies, and preparing synthesis reports which bring out the policy proposals that members presented. They also mediate to reconcile opposing views and support members in reaching compromises. 'They are our technical assistance', in one member's words.

This level of involvement allows members to have complete control over the positions adopted, ensures transparency, and fits Oxfam's position as co-ordinator of the national campaign. Members of the alliance still feel the need for regular background information and documentation specifically on the political and social context and labour issues in the country; and for regular brainstorming sessions that help reflect on long- and short-term policy objectives. Working through these processes ensures that the alliance doesn't jump immediately from the problem to a long-term solution, and identifies short-term winnable steps that are a necessary intermediate part of the overall process.

The alliance in Nicaragua, having gathered evidence and opinions from women workers about its proposed national occupational health and safety law, passed the proposals to MEC's legal team to formulate the final version in the technical and legal language that is required for official documents. This bill was presented to the National Assembly; but they have not passed it yet. However, the members of the alliance are also members of the National Council for Occupational Health and Safety, and this council did contribute to the National Strategic Plan for Occupational Health and Safety, published by the Ministry of Labour at the end of 2004. It could be argued that the campaign created a favourable environment for this, although the plan was not a focus of the campaign.

MEC also developed a comprehensive proposal for a national employment policy which would include: a legal framework to guarantee women's entry into the workplace with salaries that meet basic needs; accessible credit programmes for small businesses; government mechanisms to distribute and legalise the ownership of land; the creation of child-development centres in businesses where more than 25 women are employed, in order to guarantee a safe place for their children and the possibility of breast-feeding for babies; and better training and technical education for women. These policies were presented to the president of Nicaragua in March 2006, during the Eighth Colloquium in Managua with 1,500 women present. The president, with all these women as witnesses, ordered the labour minister to incorporate MEC's proposal into the national policy being developed by the labour minister. The policy was announced on 1 May 2006.

As a further example of the alliance's pro-active and co-operative approach to its targets, it suggested to the government and the business community the need to provide healthy working environments as a way of contributing to greater productivity from women workers, as well as a reduction in staff turnover. Although staff turnover is not a concern that has been publicly expressed by company representatives, MEC believes it is worthwhile to raise this issue, to make employers think about the need to keep workers who have accumulated experience, and so maintain productivity and reduce production costs.

In Sri Lanka, the process of agreeing a policy position was valuable not just for its outcome, but also as a way of cementing a fragile alliance. In October 2003, the alliance had a two-day meeting to prioritise and pick one or two issues that they could campaign on. The participants finally came up with a list of four issues or demands: respect for freedom of association; compensation for workers who had lost their jobs; paying living wages; and improving living conditions in the overcrowded 'dormitories' for migrant workers.

A previously disparate group, each working individually in different areas of interest and coming together occasionally, they now had four common areas of work. Continuous participative discussions concerning campaign issues, along with a constant flow of information in the local language, made it possible for organisations to become truly involved in designing the campaign. Through a consultative decision-making process, the alliance decided on common objectives and a detailed campaign plan, allocating joint responsibility to all partners involved in carrying out the campaign activities. Organisations that were used to tackling one issue at a time, as and when it arose, were made to focus on long-term campaign objectives and activities.

The targets for the four demands were the employers, buyers, government authorities, and other international campaigns. At the same time, employers (and, of course, workers) were affected by the phase-out of the MFA, as described earlier. This gave the alliance another policy focus, to alert the government to the impact of the phase-out on the workers who lost jobs. ALaRM was the key voice to bring the attention of the Department of Labour to the situation of *workers* within the industry, not just the situation of the industry owners. In this, the alliance adopted a co-operative stance towards the government and, by implication, towards the employers.

In Colombia, the focus on Law 789 seems to have been self-evident from the beginning of the alliance. The campaign concentrated on denouncing the law and showing how it had affected women workers. The alliance also identified the *Comisión de Seguimiento y Verificación de Políticas de Empleo* (Follow-up and Verification Commission on Employment Policies), created in Law 789 itself, as an instrument for oversight and for political action (something which the trade unions on their own had not noticed). Consistent with this reactive, defensive approach to policy, the alliance successfully lobbied congress against a proposed change in women's retirement age. The initiative came from the government; the alliance, rather than campaigning for an improvement in the conditions of women workers, was campaigning against a worsening of their conditions. The alliance also argued for a referendum on the proposed free trade agreement with the USA; once again, they were reacting to an initiative from the government, but the idea of a referendum is a useful device to keep the debate going and create space for counter-arguments. The internal debate within the alliance was more concerned with gender-equality issues. Women's Dialogues – *Los Diálogos de Mujeres*, promoted by the campaign, became a space for open debate within the alliance, with which it sought to strengthen the environment of trust within the campaign. These events proved fruitful and increased the respect and recognition that male leaders gave to the women leaders of the alliance.

Publication

Some alliances published the results of their research (as in Sri Lanka and the USA) or their policy making. As noted previously, the Moroccan alliance produced a brochure in March 2005, which included an analysis of the labour code, testimonies from women workers, and the alliance's policy agenda. This was widely distributed to authorities, private-sector actors, and union members. They were also able to distribute the brochure at events such as International Women's Day.

For the Moroccan alliance, preparing the brochure was the 'excuse' or 'trigger' that got everyone thinking about developing common policy. The alliance existed, and everyone had ideas about what needed to change in order to improve women workers' rights, but all discussions had been oral and there was no way to present the alliance's messages to campaign targets and the public. It was a very helpful exercise to pull together everyone's ideas, to have a group discussion about how to prioritise proposals, and to write everything down. Writing down everyone's ideas on paper allowed the group to prioritise messages and to see what they had in common. Once common policy was agreed, having it produced in a brochure

80

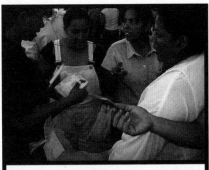

Informing women of their rights – women campaigners handing out health and safety pamphlets to workers as they leave a free trade zone in Nicaragua.
Source: MEC, 2004

gave alliance members a feeling of ownership and pride: 'this is our message and we are conveying it to the world clearly and effectively'.

The Nicaraguan campaign published and distributed leaflets on health and safety to over 10,000 workers. In Colombia, for every big campaign event, a leaflet or pamphlet was produced for distribution to the attending public. Sri Lanka has produced a study related to living wages.

There are two helpful side effects of publishing your policy. The fact that the policy is to be printed up and distributed gives greater focus to the discussions that create the policy; and once it is published there is a greater incentive for all the members of the alliance to stick with the agreed policy proposal.

International

A few members of some alliances participated in international conferences. This gave them an opportunity to describe the context and content of their own campaign, and to learn from campaigns in other countries, whether similar or very different. The Moroccan alliance found that international conferences and seminars helped to exchange ideas and views with other countries facing similar problems. It was also a good group exercise for strengthening relations between alliance members, as they needed to work together to prepare their participation in a conference. Members felt that the chance to assume the responsibility of representing the alliance in a conference was also good because it increased their feeling of ownership and enhanced their commitment. The alliance has learnt that participation in conferences/seminars should be targeted and relate directly to the campaign's strategy, in order to have an added value for the campaign. The alliance participated in two conferences in 2005: in Barcelona, Spain, and in Rabat, Morocco. Both had participants from Mediterranean countries (European and Arab).

Members of the Colombian alliance travelled even more widely: to Ecuador and Argentina in 2005 and to Venezuela in 2006. The individuals who travelled reported similar benefits to their self-confidence and learning.

National campaigns took place in the context of international research and policy making. Oxfam supplied the alliance in Morocco with three types of documentation: updates on other Oxfam-linked campaigns, research on the textiles sector and Spanish brands in Morocco (as mentioned above), and global research such as the 'Trading Away Our Rights' report. Although, as mentioned earlier, the members of the alliance appreciated information about international experiences and perspectives while designing their campaign strategy, the same could not be said for the process of developing alternative policy proposals. The members of the alliance did not see documentation on campaigns in other countries as particularly useful for developing policy proposals in their own country, as it was always in English and members could not relate to the cases presented – 'experiences from other countries are not very useful; there are different cases and contexts requiring different approaches'. On the contrary, documentation on the textiles sector in Morocco, translated into French, was seen as more interesting and useful, but again not essential to the campaign's messaging. Finally, documentation from Oxfam's global research was seen as generally interesting, but not useful when trying to define specific demands to the local government, adapted to the local context. Judging from past experience, new documentation would need to be accompanied by a presentation and a group discussion, in order to relate the topic to the country-level situation and to familiarise the alliance with the analysis. It would also help if the document were translated into Arabic.

The campaign in Nicaragua was planned in an international context. It started with regional (Central American) meetings, followed by research compiled from four national pieces of research, then a regional decision on focus and slogan, and moved to implementation nationally. Occupational health and safety was defined as the key focus of the campaign, based on the results of research in the region. This research investigated working conditions in factories in special industrial zones, especially those conditions that affect women. National studies carried out in Honduras, Guatemala, El Salvador, and Nicaragua confirmed these findings.

Summary

It is not always essential to develop complete legitimate, acceptable, alternative policy proposals. If you don't develop policy, you must develop a proposition for change – for instance in the practice of businesses or employers. FLOC, in the USA, simply ignored the legal framework for labour rights, despite its inadequacies, concluding that it could achieve more for migrant workers by focusing on employers' practice. The alliance in Colombia criticised Law 789, opposed changes in women's retirement age, and called for a referendum on the free trade proposal – leaving it to the government to come up with better ideas and justify the free trade agreement. The alliances in Sri Lanka and Morocco used the policy-formulation process as an alliance-building exercise, and adopted, for the time being, a co-operative stance towards their respective governments. The Moroccan alliance did not address employers directly; the Sri Lankan alliance agreed a list of four demands to employers. The Nicaraguan alliance had the most pro-active approach to policy, and actually drafted legislation for congress to consider.

All the alliances conducted or used research, though not always to feed into a policy-making process. The alliance in Sri Lanka found that the provision of balanced research from a worker perspective also helps to increase credibility and gain recognition.

Key points

- Move beyond identifying problems to developing and proposing alternatives, including policy solutions, in order to be taken seriously. By formulating proposals, you can lead the debates and set the agenda, instead of just reacting to others' proposals.

- Explain your analysis to others: this can clarify the thinking of the alliance and make developing a policy proposal easier.

- Bear in mind that developing a policy proposal can focus the discussions within the alliance, and clarify what members are really willing to campaign for.

- Remember that the policy – or proposition for change – that the alliance develops may influence its strategy in relation to the campaign targets (whether to be co-operative or confrontational).

- Choose if, when, and how to publish policy proposals, according to whom the alliance wishes to inform. In any case, explain the policy proposal clearly and briefly, with details about who to contact for further information.

- Consider whether the alliance may benefit from international research and published information from around the world, to put the essence of your proposal in context, with global backing.

Conclusion

Many organisations, including the ones that make up the alliances described in this book, start their work to change the world by organising strategies, carrying out awareness-raising activities, and undertaking capacity-building programmes. At some point, the organisations in this book decided that they wanted to try a new way of working, and take a new step to strengthen their work, because they felt that campaigning would be a good method to achieve the changes that they wanted. Community organisations, as well as non-government organisations and trade unions, can have little experience in campaigning, and this can be paralysing. The stories in this book describe the ups and downs, the steps forward and the setbacks, of organisations just like yours.

We cannot change the world without understanding it, and we cannot plan effective campaigns without understanding how campaigns work in very complex situations. This factual and descriptive text is intended to provide background to the processes and relationships that were built, context for the difficult decisions and choices that the alliances made, and justification for the key points of advice given at the end of each chapter. These, in turn, are intended to be useful for organisations which are carrying out or planning to carry out a campaign.

Having said that, there are key lessons that can be drawn from these experiences, no matter their context:

- campaigning is a long-term process;
- innovation, imagination, flexibility, patience, and persistence are all valuable qualities;
- alliances are necessary and effective, even though they may be hard work;
- a clear strategy will facilitate an effective campaign;
- alliances should use every possible means to communicate to all relevant audiences;

- changing ideas and beliefs is as important as changing policy and practice;
- all campaigns, even if not explicitly proposed to be about women's rights, should be informed by a rigorous gender analysis before research is done and before strategies are defined.

The reality is that it is hard work to make change happen. It is equally true, though, that the very attempt teaches us all skills that we can use over and over again, in each new effort. The stories in this book show us that change happens when people work together. The women and migrant workers in these campaigns show us that change can come from all quadrants. It is imperative that we rise to the challenge to overcome the histories and experiences that divide us. Above all, we must remember that the ideals of justice and development are worth all the hard work of campaigning.

Notes

1 Freedom of association is defined by the International Labour Organisation as the right of workers and employers to form and join organisations of their own choosing, and it is enshrined as a core labour standard in International Labour Conventions 87 and 98. It is a pre-requisite for sound collective bargaining and social dialogue.

2 For further information see: www.ilo.org/public/english/bureau/inf.download/women/pdf/factsseet.pdf.

3 Oxfam (2004) 'Trading Away Our Rights: Women Working in Global Supply Chains', Oxford: Oxfam, available at: http://publications.oxfam.org.uk/oxfam/display.asp?K=184019537585413&sf_01=CTITLE&st_01=trading+away+our+rights&sort=SORT_DATE%2FD&m=2&dc=6.

4 The information about the Gini Co-efficient is from the UN Development Programme and can be found at: http://hdr.undp.org/hdr2006/statistics/indicators/147.html.

5 *Maquila* is a term widely used across Latin America; it means a particular type of factory often under international ownership, sometimes in conjunction with a national company interest – an assembly plant, usually located in export-processing zones, where products such as garments and electronics are put together from imported pieces.

6 See H. P. Lankes (2002) 'Market access for developing countries', Finance & Development 39 (3), available at: www.imf.org/external/pubs/ft/fandd/2002/09/lankes.htm.

86

Appendix • The alliance members

Colombia

Aprodic

Asomujer & Trabajo

Casa de la Mujer

Cemci

Central General del Trabajo

Central Unitaria de Trabajadores

Centro Cultural Popular Meléndez

Centro Estudios del Trabajo

Cetec

Colectivo Mujer y Calidad de Vida

Comisión Colombiana de Juristas

Comité Cívico de Fredonia

Confederación de Trabajadores de
Colombia

Corpomujer

Corporación Cactus

Corporación Centro Convivamos

Corporación Centro de Acciones Integrales
para la Mujer, Cami

Corporación Educativa Combos

Corporación Región

Corporación Sisma Mujer

Corporación Vamos Mujer

CUT –Antioquia

CUT – Comité Operativo Bolívar

CUT, Valle, Departamento de la mujer

Escuela Nacional Sindical ENS

Fundación Nueva República

FUNSAREP

Grupo de Apoyo Pedagógico

Hogar Juvenil

Instituto Latinoamericano de Servicios
Legales Alternativos

Instituto María Cano

Instituto Popular de Capacitación

Mavi

Mujeres Que Crean

Oxfam Internacional

Paz y Bien

Red de Empoderamiento de la Mujer

Red Decide Mujer

Red Internacional de Género y Economía

Red Nacional de Mujeres – Cali

Red Nacional De Mujeres Afrocolombianas
– Kambirí

Red Viva

Semillas de Mostaza

Sí Mujer

Sindicato de trabajadoras de hogares
infantiles de Bolívar Sintrahicobol

Sindicato de trabajadores y empleados públicos universitarios de Colombia, Sintraunicol, seccional Cartagena

Sutev, Secretaría de asuntos de la mujer

Taller Abierto

Tribunal Nacional Mujeres y DESC

Unión de Ciudadanas de Colombia

Unión de Empelaos Bancarios

Universidad de La Salle

Utrahogar

Morocco

Association Marocaine de Droits de la Femme

Association Marocaine de Droits Humains

Centre des Droits des Gens

Confédération Démocratique du Travail

Ligue Démocratique des Droits des Femmes

Union Marocaine du Travail

Nicaragua

Central Sandinista de Trabajadores José Benito Escobar

Centro Humboldt

Instituto Nicaraguense de Seguridad Social

Movimiento de Mujeres Trabajadoras y Desempleadas María Elena Cuadra (MEC)

Ministerio de Salud

Ministerio de Trabajo

Organización Panamericana de Salud

Universidad Nacional Autonoma de Nicaragua (León y Managua)

Sri Lanka

All Ceylon Federation of Free Trade Unions

American Centre for International Labour Solidarity

Dabindu Collective Women's Organisation

Free Trade Zone & General Services Workers Union

Friedrich Ebert Stiftung

Jathika Sevaka Sangamaya

Right to Life Labour NGO

Sri Lanka Nidahas Sevaka Sangamaya

United Federation of Labour

Women's Centre Women's Organisation

Young Christian Workers

USA

The members of the alliance in the USA were so numerous that they are not listed here for reasons of space.

Resources

This section is a useful starting point for further research and exploration. It lists useful web resources, books, papers and articles, grouped under the five chapter topics in the book. There is also an additional section on fundraising and a list of Oxfam contact details. The section is not designed to be fully comprehensive, but rather offers a range of further reference points for the interested reader.

Please note that the book also has a **companion website**, available at: www.oxfam.org.uk/nationalcampaigns. This site contains further photos from the five case-study campaigns, video clips, campaigning materials, and a set of PowerPoint slides which can be used to help promote the book to new readers.

Building alliances

Books, papers, reports, articles

D. Eade and A. Leather (eds.), 'Part 1: Alliances and Tensions between Labor Unions and NGOs', in D. Eade and A. Leather (eds.) *Development NGOs and Labor Unions*, Bloomfield, CT: Kumarian Press, Inc, 2005.

> An academic look at alliances between organisations at a global and a local level, presented through a series of articles. This provides a top-line study of the types of challenges that organisations will need to consider as they begin to forge alliances and networks.

G. Gordon, *Advocacy Toolkit: Practical Action for Advocacy*, Teddington: Tearfund, 2002.

> The second book in an advocacy series, this resource provides tips for action in campaigning. From identifying the issue, building alliances with communities, researching, and preparing a strategic plan to bringing it all together in an action campaign, this toolkit offers 36 specific skill-building tools and examples. http://tilz.tearfund.org/webdocs/Tilz/Roots/English/Advocacy%20toolkit/Advocacy%20toolkit_E_FULL%20DOC_Part%20C.pdf

The Policy Project, *Networking for Policy Change: An Advocacy Training Manual*, Washington, DC: The Futures Group International, 1999.

> This manual is organised as a self-study guide to learning advocacy. Its intention is to train the reader how to create advocacy networks and strategise successful campaigns through a step-by-step process of building skills through instruction and reflection. The focus of the publication is public-health campaigning, but the skills and supporting principles are transferable to all categories of campaigning organisations.
> www.policyproject.com/pubs/AdvocacyManual.pdf

Web resources

Asian Pacific American Labor Alliance (APALA) Chapter Toolkit, Washington, DC: APALA, 2006.

> This toolkit is an organisation-specific manual that offers general advice about creating an alliance within a larger movement. Though focused on developed-country organisational alliances, a number of the ideas, tools, and worksheets could be modified to apply to connections between groups in lesser-developed country contexts as well.
> www.apalanet.org/ht/a/GetDocumentAction/id/12103

Civil Society Research and Support Collective, a series of publications for garment workers in Africa, produced for International Textile, Garment and Leather Workers' Federation (www.itglwf.org) by Civil Society Research and Support Collective (www.csrsc.org.za), South Africa: Prontaprint (no copyright), 2005.

> This series of booklets was designed as an educational tool for organisations working to improve labour conditions in multi-national corporations in Africa. Book One provides a background to the campaign. Book Two approaches the methodology behind creating local and international links in the formal and informal sectors. Book Three is a workbook of activities and case studies intending to inspire discussion and innovation around campaigns in this sector.
>
> Book One 'Asian Multinationals in Africa, information and strategy guide'
> www.somo.nl/html/paginas/pdf/Garment_workers_africa_booklet1_EN.pdf
> Book Two 'Organizing and campaigning: developing union strategy and capacity'
> www.somo.nl/html/paginas/pdf/Garment_workers_africa_booklet2_EN.pdf
> Book Three 'A story of organising, a shopfloor workbook'
> www.somo.nl/html/paginas/pdf/Garment_workers_africa_booklet3_EN.pdf

Developing a strategy

Books, papers, reports, articles

D. Cohen, R. de la Vega, and G. Watson, *Advocacy for Social Justice: A Global Action and Reflection Guide*, Oxfam America, The Advocacy Institute, and Kumarian Press, Inc., 2001. Spanish: D. Cohen, R. de la Vega, R., y G. Watson, *Incidencia para la Justicia Social: Guía Global de Acción y Reflexión*, Oxfam America y Advocacy Institute, Abya-Yala, Quito, Ecuador, 2004.

> Intended for the advocacy practitioner and trainer alike, this book explores the elements of advocacy and offers a toolkit for taking action, comprehensive case studies, and further resource listings for activists around the world.

T. Kingham and J. Coe, *The Good Campaigns Guide: Campaigning for Impact*, London: NCVO, 2005.

> This book outlines the entire campaign cycle from the standpoint of making an impact. Every stage is explained in regards to how the campaigner can make change happen. This is followed by a detailed description of what makes a good campaigning organisation. This resource is easy-to-follow and well-informed and makes the most of examples, charts, and checklists to facilitate understanding of campaigning principles.

M. Lattimer, *The Campaigning Handbook: Second Edition*, London: The Directory of Social Change, 2000.

> This resource is UK-focused and less applicable globally than the other resources in this section. Chapter 16 'Campaign strategy', however, is universally applicable. The content is applicable to both beginner and expert campaigners and develops the theoretical aspect of strategy rather than the practical.

Maquila Solidarity Network, *Brand Campaigns and Worker Organizing*, Toronto: Maquila Solidarity Network, 2005.

> Three case studies of successful international campaigns on labour rights. They are available in Spanish. Order from:
> http://en.maquilasolidarity.org/sites/maquilasolidarity.org/files/Ordering BrandCampaignsWorkerOrganizing-1bis.pdf

Web resources

Amnesty International, *Campaigning Manual*, London: Amnesty International Publications, 2001.

> A comprehensive resource that, despite being written specifically for Amnesty International campaigners, provides a number of practical resources. Most useful to a beginner campaigner is Section 2, which includes advice on campaigning techniques, working with the media, preparing campaign materials, outreach, and lobbying.
> www.amnesty.org/resources/pdf/campaigning-manual/campaigning-manual.pdf

R. Sharma, *An Introduction to Advocacy: Training Guide*, Washington, DC: Support for Analysis and Research in Africa.

> A training guide divided into ten modules covering themes from answering the question, 'What is Advocacy?' to developing strategies, building alliances, and fundraising techniques. Each module contains a step-by-step path to achieving defined objectives and includes definitions and helpful hints along the way. www.aed.org/ToolsandPublications/upload/PNABZ919.pdf

W. Thys (ed.), *10 Trade Union Actions to strengthen the status of workers in the informal sector*, published for the Verba Informal Economy programme, Brussels, 2004.

> A manual intended to provide theoretical, practical, and strategic solutions to organising and strategising a campaign for improved legal status of workers. It includes practical exercises to strengthen understanding of the material and presents detailed case studies of labour-rights initiatives across three continents. www.cmt-wcl.org/cmt/ewcm.nsf/0/2e1580062c589391c1256eb300535f09/$file/ wva-infecon-en.pdf?openelement
> Spanish: www.cmt-wcl.org/cmt/ewcm.nsf/0/aef9e434de0d2500c125eb300538aca/ $file/wva-infecon-sp.pdf?openelement

Incorporating gender-equality work

Books, papers, reports, articles

C. Datar, 'Deterrents in organizing women tobacco workers in Nipani', in S. Wieringa (ed.) *Subversive Women: Women's Movements in Africa, Asia, Latin America and the Caribbean*, New Delhi: KALI for Women, 1995.

A first-person narrative from the perspective of a researcher about the progress of the unions in Nipani. Difficulties faced by the unions are analysed, and suggestions for future strategising are proposed in the context of the difficulties of changing attitudes and putting ideas into practice.

K. Evans, 'A guide to feminist advocacy', in K. Kingma and C. Sweetman (eds.) *Gender, Development, and Advocacy*, Oxford: Oxfam Publishing, 2005.

Developed from Evans' work with the Association for Women's Rights in Development (www.awid.org/publications/primers/waysmeans1.pdf), this chapter focuses specifically on weaving women-centred concerns into general campaigning. Citing a number of case studies both successful and disastrous, this chapter succeeds in offering a broad view of advocacy and advocacy strategies. In addition, Evans offers practical advice on negotiating advocacy space and presents questions to consider when assessing a strategy, both before and after implementation.

Web resources

Centre for Development and Population Activities, *Cairo, Beijing, and Beyond:
A Handbook on Advocacy for Women Leaders*, Washington, DC: CEDPA, 1995.
>A developing-country focused handbook for advocacy with an emphasis on supporting women who are in the forefront of the campaign. This manual clearly delineates objectives for successful advocacy, offers practical tips, and is supplemented by a wealth of profiles of female advocates, their work, and their contact information.
>www.womensciencenet.org/admin/media/588458632726e1f0ddf786f715a19744040248.pdf

Global Unions' Organising Campaign, *Campaign Kit*.
>A campaign kit with a focus on organising women workers and increasing women's participation in unions. It also provides practical advice on creating campaign action plans and numerous resources and contacts.
>ww.icftu.org/www/pdf/u4w-campaignkit-en.pdf
>Spanish: www.icftu.org/www/pdf/u4w-campaignkit-es.pdf

Negotiating Better Working and Living Conditions – Gender Mainstreaming in Collective Bargaining
>A series of four booklets published by the World Confederation of Labour with an emphasis on collective bargaining on local and global levels, and a focus on eastern and central European states. The goal of this collection is to encourage unions to consider gender in their negotiating and to provide a toolkit for incorporating the gender dimension into all aspects of lobbying work.
>Booklet 1 'Company Level'
>www.cmt-wcl.org/cmt/ewcm.nsf/0/5c4b11f26a988414c1256feb00371a9c/$file/icftu-wclmanual-booklet%201.pdf?openelement
>Booklet 2 'Over the Company Walls'
>www.cmt-wcl.org/cmt/ewcm.nsf/0/935927cc2f7b5311c1256feb003748eb/$file/icftu-wclmanual-booklet%202.pdf?openelement
>Booklet 3 'Collective Negotiating at the European and Global Level'
>www.cmt-wcl.org/cmt/ewcm.nsf/0/62d1d7c6680e956cc1257083002f2679/$file/icftu-wclmanual-booklet%203.pdf?openelement
>Booklet 4 'Strategy and Techniques of Negotiations'
>www.cmt-wcl.org/cmt/ewcm.nsf/0/20249dd5d64413d2c1256feb00375a15/$file/icftu-wclmanual-booklet%204.pdf?openelement

'Working with Men for Women's Rights', *Young Women and Leadership* Number 2, February 2004.

> A globally applicable article geared at a) convincing women's groups of the importance of working with male-dominated organisations and b) instructing women on the best way to incorporate working with men in their organisations. Serving as a primer for integration, this article touches briefly on gender sensitisation for both sides as well as the importance of being aware of perceived gender roles and using this knowledge to create an appropriate dual-gender working space.
> www.awid.org/publications/primers/waysmeans2.pdf
> Spanish: www.awid.org/publications/primers/waysmeanssp2.pdf

Using the media

Books, papers, reports, articles

S. Gregory, *Video for change: a guide for Advocacy and Activism*, London: Pluto Press, 2005.

> A forward-looking book which explores the arena of using video as evidence, as persuasion, and as a story-telling tool. It is not overly focused on the technical aspect. Gregory discusses important decisions such as how to determine whether video will be an asset to a campaign and how to reach key audiences through strategic distribution.

A. McKinley, *Building a Media Strategy for Political Advocacy*, Washington, DC: Washington Office on Latin America, 2002.

> This is a manual for integrating media into campaigns for policy reform. It contains theoretical and practical direction for creating plans and media strategies. Though this has a Central American focus, many of the concepts and skills are transferable to other situations.
> Spanish: www.wola.org/media/atp_construyendo_estrategia_de_medios_jul_05.pdf

D. Jones, *Banners and Dragons*, London: Amnesty International UK, 2003.

> A brief full-colour guide to low-cost, impressive, media interest-catching campaign techniques produced by Amnesty International UK. Detailed instructions provided for each suggestion.

K. Wolf, *Now Hear This: The Nine Laws of Successful Advocacy Communications*, Washington, DC: Fenton Communications, 2001.

> This is a short, clearly written, full-colour introduction to communicating as an advocate. Using input from 25 leaders in communications, the pamphlet sets out common-sense laws with brief references to real situations to illustrate the point.
> www.fenton.com/pages/5_resources/pdf/Packard_Brochure.pdf

Web resources

Boulle, J. and D. Newton, *MDG Campaigning Toolkit*, CIVICUS: World Alliance for Citizen Participation and MDG Campaign Office.
> A toolkit which focuses on the Millennium Development Goals but which provides general information and practical examples of campaigning techniques in a global context. Each aspect of campaigning is explained in a detailed, informative manner, often supported by illustrations and case studies.
> Chapter 3 'Campaigning toolkit'
> www.civicus.org/mdg/3-1.htm
> Chapter 4 'Campaigning tools'
> www.civicus.org/mdg/4-1.htm
> Chapter 5 'Campaign skills'
> www.civicus.org/mdg/5-1.htm

Latin America Solidarity Coalition, 'Preparing for an interview', 2003.
> This brief article consists of a checklist of key things to remember before, during, and after an interview.
> www.lasolidarity.org/Media/preparingforaninterview.htm

Forces for Change – Informal Economy Organisations in Africa, War on Want (WoW), Workers Education Association Zambia (WEAZ), Alliance for Informal Economy Associations (AZIEA), 2006.
> Chapter 5 presents case studies on informal sector organisation and strategising advocacy campaigns. Appendix 4 provides a list of trade unions and associations in Africa, organised by country.
> www.waronwant.org/download.php?id=421
> www.waronwant.org/download.php?id=422

Human Rights Video Project.
> The organisation's mission is to increase public awareness of rights issues using documentary films. Their website includes a collection of video used as an advocacy technique in labour-rights issues as well as links to related organisations and campaigns.
> www.humanrightsproject.org/vid_detail.php?film_id=1&asset=film_resources

Pressureworks/Christian Aid, *How to write a press release*, 2006.
> A quick, easy-to-follow guide with top tips on how to write a press release and the importance of having a dialogue with the media.
> www.pressureworks.org/usefulstuff/how/release.html

World Comics, *How to Make Campaign Comics*, 2005.
> A simple, easy-to-follow list of suggestions for using comics to promote a campaign or an organisation. The site includes a number of examples of both grassroots and campaign comic strips and videos as well as case studies that focus on the process of incorporating comics into a campaign.
> www.worldcomics.fi/howto_campaign.shtml

World Development Movement

> This is an active global campaigning organisation with a number of useful materials. Of primary interest are the video examples of campaigning stunts and events intended to influence the media. The link below takes you directly to videos, many of which focus not only on the event, but also on the background and its preparation.
> www.wdm.org.uk/resources/multimedia/video.htm

Developing policy

Books, papers, reports, articles

J. Chapman and T. Fisher, 'The effectiveness of NGO campaigning', in *Development and Practice* 10:2 (151–65), 2000.

> Taking case studies of two campaigns run locally in Ghana and India, this article attempts to answer questions regarding the trend for NGOs to campaign on policies according to their relevance, effectiveness, and impact. This article concludes with the various limitations of campaigning but also states how campaigns can be a success at a number of levels. A practical, in-depth look at campaigns, policy, and whether it effects change on the ground.

F. Dodds and M. Strauss, *How to Lobby at Intergovernmental Meetings*, London: Earthscan Publications Ltd., 2004.

> This book approaches the subject of intergovernmental lobbying from both a governmental and non-governmental stakeholder perspective. The stated intent of the book is to allow the lobbyer to maximise their resources by providing an understanding of how intergovernmental meetings work and how best to approach the lobbying process.

A. Gienapp, J. Reisman, and S. Stachowiak, *A Guide to Measuring Advocacy and Policy*, Baltimore, MD: Annie E. Casey Foundation, 2007.

> Researched and written by Organizational Research Services (www.organizationalresearch.com), this is an innovative and practical guide to measuring the efficacy of advocacy and policy. Written with an all-encompassing view, the three sections are specifically designed for individuals at various places on the advocacy ladder. This work fills a gap as regards applying evaluation and measurements to overall campaign-strategy techniques, particularly influencing policy. The examples are US-specific, but the theory and direction is globally applicable.
> www.organizationalresearch.com/publications/a_guide_to_measuring_advocacy _and_policy.pdf

Web resources

CAFOD, ChristianAid, Trocaire, *Monitoring Government Policies: A Toolkit for Civil Society Organizations in Africa.*
> A toolkit that assists organisations in identifying which government policies to research and how to use this information to campaign for change. It serves as a workbook as well as a reference to related resources and background information regarding techniques and processes.
> http://trocaire.org/pdfs/policy/governance/monitoringgovernmentpolicies.pdf

A. Carbert, 'Learning from Experience: Activist Reflections on 'Insider-Outsider' Strategies', in *Spotlight*, Number 4, 2004.
> An occasional paper released by the Association for Women's Rights in Development (AIWD – www.awid.org) in which the focus is on establishing the different strategies involved once activism enters the policy sphere. Through ten interviews with activists from around the world, Carbert explores the importance of strategy and of communication when attempting to bridge the gap between social change and policy-making.
> www.awid.org/publications/OccasionalPapers/spotlight4_en.pdf

Fundraising

J. Barbato and D. Furlich, *Writing for a Good Cause: The Complete Guide to Crafting Proposals and Other Persuasive Pieces for Nonprofits*, New York: Fireside, 2000.
> A wittily written guide to preparing grant proposals, newsletters, electronic communications, and other forms of persuasive writing. It covers everything from getting started, what to include, and what to do when things go wrong. Though written with Western non-profits in mind, the sound advice is applicable to any organisation.

K. Klein, 'The ten most important things you can know about fundraising', *Grassroots Fundraising Journal* 1, 2004.
> www.grassrootsfundraising.org/howto/v23_n1_art03.pdf

K. Klein (ed.) 'Cómo Recaudar Fondos en su Comunidad' (How to Raise Money in Your Community)
> Selected articles from the Grassroots Fundraising Journal focusing on basic fundraising skills. The value of these suggestions is that they do not rely on technical knowledge or even expensive equipment or computers; instead the focus is on building relationships and fundraising at a local level.
> Spanish: www.grassrootsfundraising.org/magazine/collections.html#como

A. Robinson and K. Klein, *Grassroots Grants: An Activist's Guide to Proposal Writing*, San Francisco: JosseyBass, 1996.

A basic guide to grants from a grassroots perspective, this guide uses four case studies to demonstrate how to find the money and how to get the funding needed.

Oxfam contact details

Oxfam International and Affiliates

Suite 20, 266 Banbury Road, Oxford, OX2 7DL, UK
Tel: +44 1865 339 100
Fax: +44 1865 339 101
Email: information@oxfaminternational.org
Website: www.oxfam.org; www.oxfam.org/es/

Oxfam America: www.oxfamamerica.org; www.oxfamamerica.org/es/
Oxfam Australia: www.oxfam.org.au/
Oxfam-in-Belgium: www.oxfamsol.be
Oxfam Canada: www.oxfam.ca
Oxfam France (Agir ici): www.oxfamfrance.org
Oxfam Germany: www.oxfam.de
Oxfam Great Britain: www.oxfam.org.uk
Oxfam Hong Kong: www.oxfam.org.hk
Intermón Oxfam: www.intermonoxfam.org
Oxfam Ireland: www.oxfamireland.org
Oxfam New Zealand: www.oxfam.org.nz
Oxfam Novib (Netherlands): www.oxfamnovib.nl; www.oxfamnovib.nl/id.html?id=3734&lang=es
Oxfam Québec: www.oxfam.qc.ca

Index